D0481299

"*Carrots and Sticks Don't Work* brings a clear understanding to leadership by providing very useful methods that will enable managers of people to connect with today's evolutionary workforce. As someone who has managed people for over thirty years and uses engagement surveys in determining employee satisfaction, I can affirm that Dr. Marciano's book is a wonderful primer for all who lead people in today's world."

> —*Diane Piraino-Koury, Owner/Operator,*
> *McDonald's Restaurant*

"I plan on having all members of my management organization read *Carrots and Sticks Don't Work*. The RESPECT Model is an easy-to-use process with many examples. I personally plan on using it both inside and outside of work!"

> —*Jack Lally, Senior Manager, FedEx*

"This book is a concise blueprint for creating a positive, cohesive workforce."

> —*A. Michael Hopp, Senior Vice President of Human*
> *Resources, Mannington Mills, Inc.*

"Finally, a book that conveys the key to employee motivation in our contemporary workplace. The RESPECT Model explicitly shows that when people are treated with respect they engage and work harder to achieve the goals of the organization."

> —*Arnold Endick, Workplace Environmental Analyst,*
> *U.S. Postal Service, Retired*

"Dr. Marciano encourages us to look at today's challenging reality through a new lens, and we emerge renewed and refreshed."

> —*Eva G. Carmichael, Internal Consultant,*
> *Superior Court of New Jersey*

"*Carrots and Sticks Don't Work* is a practical guide and reminder of how we should all behave in both our professional and personal lives. I think it's a must read and one that will become a reference for anyone that is interested in becoming a leader, becoming a better leader, or knowing what to look for in a good leader."

> —*Dave Hickey, CEO, Lumeta Corporation*

More Advance Praise for
Carrots and Sticks Don't Work

"*Carrots and Sticks Don't Work* is a profound book about the power of respect. In today's world, where ethics and consideration are at an all-time low, Dr. Marciano has written a testament to what we all need to remember: personal responsibility that earns respect."

—Jane Boucher, author of How to Love the Job You Hate

"Dr. Marciano's new book is loaded with compelling and relevant case studies, which will inspire current and future leaders with new insight and a road map for getting teams to make things happen!"

—Tony Hurst, Manager Service Operations,
Honeywell International

"Dr. Marciano goes right to the heart of true leadership. Many leaders can get short-term results through the traditional model of rewards and punishment. But true sustainable impact and results come from building respect."

—Garrett Ingram, AVP Managed Markets Strategy,
Novo Nordisk Inc.

"Outstanding! An excellent guide to help both managers and individual contributors understand what employee engagement is and why having it is critical for individuals and organizations to thrive."

—Michael Stallard, author of Fired Up or Burned Out

"In my thirty-plus years in HR, I had not read an HR book before that I would have said was a 'must have' textbook for any line manager . . . but this is one!"

—Clinton Wingrove, EVP and Principal Consultant,
Pilat HR Solutions

"I wish this book had been written twenty years earlier. It would have saved me a lot of mistakes."

—Mark Straley, President, Ortho Clinical Diagnostics,
Johnson & Johnson

"I was barely past the R in RESPECT and couldn't wait to get back to the office to try out the suggestions laid out in this book. A must read for any manager or business owner who has ever wrestled with employee productivity issues."

—*Michael Caldwell, Co-Founder/CEO,*
GigMasters.com, Inc.

"Dr. Marciano gives great advice about what works—and what doesn't—to get maximum employee engagement and discretionary effort."

—*Christopher Rice, President and CEO,*
Blessing White, Inc.

"*Carrots and Sticks Don't Work* is an easy read and an even easier application that builds respect and dignity into everyday work life."

—*Ron Golumbeck, Vice President and Director of Human*
Resources, ITT Industrial Process

"This book is a worthwhile read for organizations large and small, executives, middle managers, supervisors, and human resource professionals. Dr. Marciano's commonsense approach is appealing in today's economy where nothing is more important than to harness the loyalty, discretionary effort, and commitment of the workforce through respect."

—*Catharine Newberry, former Chief Human Strategy*
Officer, The Medicines Company

"This is a relevant and useful book for personnel management in organizations of all sizes. The RESPECT Model is a friendly and flexible tool for building a better working environment for employees and supervisors and getting results for the organization."

—*Jose S. Azcona, President, Alianza Inmobiliaria*

"*Carrots and Sticks Don't Work* is a diamond in the rough of leadership books. Dr. Marciano not only transforms the way we think about employee engagement, but his research and insights argue for a new dawn of business where respect should live at the forefront of all of our value statements."

—*Daniel Rehal, President, Vision2Voice, Inc.*

"In *Carrots and Sticks Don't Work*, Dr. Marciano combines his real-life leadership and consulting experience with an extensive background in teaching and research to help employers create and sustain a productive workforce in the twenty-first century."

> —*Carl Sorensen, Associate VP Human Resources,*
> *University of Richmond*

"The RESPECT Model created by Dr. Marciano is the best human resource program I have ever encountered. It's a step-by-step approach in creating an engaged employee. Engaged employees are an asset to every employer and organization."

> —*Carl Resnick, owner, Flemington Department Store*

"Drawing from decades of research as well as personal and clinical experience, Dr. Marciano explains how to avoid common managerial mistakes that actually undermine employee motivation. Every manager should read this highly insightful and engaging book."

> —*Nicole Tuchinda, M.D., J.D., Associate,*
> *Ropes & Gray, LLP*

Carrots and Sticks Don't Work

Carrots
and Sticks
Don't Work

Build a Culture of Employee Engagement with the Principles of RESPECT™

Paul L. Marciano, Ph.D.

New York   Chicago   San Francisco   Lisbon   London   Madrid   Mexico City
Milan   New Delhi   San Juan   Seoul   Singapore   Sydney   Toronto

Copyright © 2010 by Paul L. Marciano. All rights reserved. Printed in the United States of America. Except as permitted under the United States Copyright Act of 1976, no part of this publication may be reproduced or distributed in any form or by any means, or stored in a database or retrieval system, without the prior written permission of the publisher.

14 15   QFR   21 20 19 18 17

ISBN   978-0-07-171401-3
MHID   0-07-171401-4

Library of Congress Cataloging-in-Publication Data

Marciano, Paul L.
        Carrots and sticks don't work : build a culture of employee engagement with the
    principles of respect / by Paul L. Marciano.
            p.   cm.
        ISBN-13: 978-0-07-171401-3
        ISBN-10: 0-07-171401-4
        1. Employee motivation.   2. Employees—Attitudes.   3. Organizational
    commitment.   I. Title.

    HF5549.5.M63M363   2010
    658.3'14—dc22   2010005407

McGraw-Hill books are available at special quantity discounts to use as premiums and sales promotions or for use in corporate training programs. To contact a representative, please e-mail us at bulksales@mcgraw-hill.com.

This book is printed on acid-free paper.

Dedicated to the one I choose every day,
Karen

Contents

Preface

O ver the past twenty years, I have dedicated my life to helping leaders increase the human capital of their organizations. During this time I have learned that relationships, both personal and professional, work only within the context of respect. Born of this concept and supported by my own research as well as studies from around the world, I developed the RESPECT Model to help organizations create cultures of respect and workforces of highly engaged employees. The model has been embraced by diverse organizations ranging in size from twenty to six hundred thousand employees, including manufacturing companies, medical practices, sales organizations, pharmaceutical companies, consulting firms, schools, and government agencies. The enthusiastic adoption and success of this model is due to its simplicity, power, effectiveness, and universal appeal. It works because all human beings desire one thing: respect.

Who Will Benefit from This Book?

This book was written for leaders at all levels who wish to engage the hearts and minds of their employees. The specific examples and strategies will help managers, supervisors, team leaders, executives, small business owners, and human resources professionals increase their organization's human capital. Whether you are a brand-new first-line supervisor or the CEO of a Fortune 500 company, the RESPECT Model will increase your leadership effectiveness and the productivity of your employees.

What You Will Learn

In reading this book, you will learn the nuts and bolts of creating an engaged workforce, specifically:

1. Why traditional reward and recognition programs fail
2. The difference between engagement and motivation
3. How increasing employee engagement adds directly to the bottom line
4. Why most approaches to increasing engagement are based on unsound research
5. How to measure employee engagement in your organization
6. The link between respect and engagement
7. The RESPECT Model
   a. The power of an "actionable philosophy"
   b. The seven drivers of RESPECT
   c. Your current leadership effectiveness in showing RESPECT

    d. Specific examples of RESPECT in action
    e. Turnkey strategies and best practices to foster a
       culture of RESPECT

By reading and applying the principles and strategies in this book you will dramatically increase the commitment, loyalty, and discretionary effort of your employees. Your people and your organization will thrive in ways that you could not even have imagined. Let the RESPECT Model do for you what it has done for so many others—help you become a highly respected leader that others want to follow.

Acknowledgments

Throughout my life I have been blessed with extraordinary teachers and mentors.

I had the honor of attending Davidson College as an undergraduate and to later serve on the faculty with those I am proud to call my mentors, colleagues, and friends. I am particularly indebted to my advisor, Professor John Kello, who first exposed me to the field of Organization Development and provided me with guidance, educational experiences, and opportunities far beyond my undergraduate years.

In the field of psychology, few are held in higher esteem than Professor Alan Kazdin, my graduate advisor at Yale University. Words cannot express my gratitude for the opportunity to work with Alan and the entire Yale Psychology faculty. I am greatly blessed and humbled for my experiences with Alan and the "dream team" at the Child Conduct Clinic. No student ever had a finer role model or received better training.

Sometimes the most important decisions in life occur before we are born. My grandfathers, Lorenzo Marciano and Ludwig Bemelmans, immigrated to the United States as young men with nothing but the dreams of building a good life for themselves and their families—even those they would never meet. It is difficult for me to comprehend their courage and strength. I owe my grandfathers a debt of gratitude that I cannot repay but only honor by making the most of the opportunities that they, as well as my grandmothers and parents, set in motion.

While I could not appreciate it as a child, I want to thank my mother and father for teaching me about respect and never tolerating disrespectful behavior. I also want to thank them for teaching me about hard work and to never take our freedoms for granted. Their extraordinary sacrifices made it possible for my brothers and me to attend college and follow our dreams. I can only hope to be as selfless and loving a parent.

This book would not have been written if it were not for my wife, Karen. She has been an inspiration and integral part of this process from proposal to final edit. I could not imagine a more loving, patient, and supportive partner and just don't know what I'd do without her.

I want to thank my clients over the past twenty years who have entrusted their most valuable resources to my care. I would like to give special thanks to Mannington Mills for their generous support of my research and acknowledge their care and commitment to their employees as exemplified by their health and wellness programming.

In all of my work as a teacher, therapist, consultant, entrepreneur, and group fitness instructor, I have sought to make a difference in the lives of others. My inspiration throughout this process has been to make the workplace a more respectful environment and to improve the quality of work life for all employees. I hope that you will bring the words on these pages to life and make a difference to the people in your organization.

Introduction

The Story That Started It All

There are times in our lives when what may appear to have been a terrible decision turns out to be a great learning experience and "blessing in disguise." Early in my career I spent three months as director of research at a small consulting firm. Although I didn't realize it at the time, this brief experience would profoundly shape my understanding of employee motivation and engagement and provide the insight that led me to create the RESPECT Model. I share some of that experience with you now in the hope that it will highlight for you the critical role respect plays in keeping employees engaged.

The Last Guy Sat There

As anyone might be, I was excited and also a bit nervous for my first day of work. I arrived forty-five minutes early and found the door locked. I waited forty-five minutes before being let in by Sherry, the company's receptionist. She asked if I had a meeting with someone. I had apparently not made much of an impression when introduced as the new director of research two weeks earlier by Mary and John, the owners of the firm. I proudly announced "I work here!" and reintroduced myself. She replied, "Oh yeah, you're the new guy" and proceeded to hang up her coat, get coffee, and begin the day's crossword puzzle at her desk.

I assumed that Mary or John would be in shortly to show me around, introduce me to the staff, and discuss more fully their specific goals and expectations. Not knowing quite what to do, and receiving no direction or assistance from Sherry, I simply waited in a chair across from her desk, which served as the reception area. After thirty minutes, I finally asked if she knew when Mary or John would be arriving. "Oh, they're not coming in today," she replied. What? Could I somehow have screwed up my starting date? Confused and embarrassed, I began to put on my jacket and leave when the office phone rang. Sherry handed it to me—it was John. He apologized for having been called away for a last-minute meeting and assured me that Sherry would take good care of me. I put Sherry back on the phone and she nodded a few times and hung up. She picked up a manila envelope that had been sitting on her desk and said, "Here are the new employee forms for you to fill out."

Recognizing that a hard surface would be useful, I asked where I might find an available desk. She walked me around the corner and said, "The last guy sat there." To the left of the desk were a few dying plants and my new officemate, TJ, who warmly introduced himself and welcomed me to the company. He then offered to take me around and introduce me to the rest of the staff. Now we were getting somewhere! As we went around the office my new team members appeared engaged in a number of different activities, including conversations on sports and stocks, surfing the Web, and playing online solitaire. There was a college intern, Elaine, who did appear to be working.

After the tour, I went back to my desk and completed the forms. I handed them to Sherry and asked if John had said what I should do next. He had not. So, I asked TJ if he needed any help. He smiled and said no. As I walked around the office reiterating my offer, I received several bemused looks and no takers. I returned to my desk and thought: Have I been inserted into a "Dilbert" cartoon?

Committed to doing something productive, I found the janitorial supplies and cleaned my desk and some bookshelves. I then picked dead leaves off the plants, gave them a good watering, and moved them closer to a sunny window. I looked at my watch and thought, "How could it only be 10:30 A.M.? What am I going to do the rest of the day?" I remembered having come across several boxes of pencils in my desk and took to sharpening them. When finished, I carefully packed the pencils back into their boxes according to their length and placed them back in my desk. It was to be one of the most satisfying and productive experiences of my tenure there.

TJ had been watching me "work" while talking to his girlfriend on the phone. When he hung up I told him that I was bored out of my mind. He suggested that I learn to pace myself. Taking pity on me, he handed me a stack of reports and said, "You can read these over for typos if you'd like." He then grabbed his coat and said that he had to run out. Running sounded like a good idea.

At noon Sherry came into my office and said that she wanted to show me something. She walked me to the front door and pointed to a small magnetic whiteboard with everyone's name written down the left side and two columns labeled "In" and "Out." My name had been added to the bottom of the list and a small magnetic circle indicated that I was "In." Everyone else's circles were in the "Out" column. Although I had actually brought my lunch, there was no way that I was staying "In" and went to move my circle to "Out." Sherry then explained that team members took turns answering the phones during her lunch break and, as I was the only one left "In," that would be me today. She put on her coat and walked out.

I prayed for the phone not to ring. Mary called first. We chatted for a minute, and then she asked me to transfer her to TJ's voice mail. Of course, I had no idea how to do that and hung up on her. Nor was I of any help to a client who called to schedule an assessment for one of his employees. "Yes," I told him, "I am new." I then did the only reasonable thing and took the phone off the hook. As I sat there, I had to consider the very real possibility that I had made a very bad decision. Six years in graduate school at Yale and here I was answering phones. I had walked away from a tenure-track position at one of the best schools in the country and was now sharpening pencils. I felt a wave of nausea rush over me and considered simply walking out and leaving a note. Of course, I would be sure to push my magnetic circle to the "Out" column.

The time from 1:00 to 5:00 passed more slowly than any previous four hours of my life. As I sat at my desk, I thought of the *Seinfeld* episode where George had gotten a job but had been given nothing to do and spent the day sharpening pencils and throwing them like darts into the fiberboard ceiling. I seriously doubted anyone would notice. I glanced over at the dying plants and realized that this was not an environment in which plants or people could thrive. At 5:00, I pushed my circle to "Out" and went home. I slept little that night as my thoughts raced between "What have I done?" and "Surely things will get better once I meet with John."

On the second day, I was the first to arrive at 8:30 and again waited for Sherry to unlock the door at 8:59. Upon seeing me, she looked surprised and said, "You're back." Apparently, she gave me more credit than I deserved. I checked "In."

I spent the first part of the morning visiting the office plants and staff. The plants seemed livelier than the day before. I could not say the same of my colleagues. I had brought in my laptop and replied to e-mails and read the news. When John checked "In" at 10:30, I felt an incredible sense of relief. He greeted me enthusiastically and congratulated me on finding my desk. I twitched as I realized that the bar was even lower than I had imagined. He told me that he had a great idea; he was taking me shopping to get office supplies for my desk. I assured him that I had plenty of well-sharpened pencils.

We retuned an hour later with several bags of supplies— almost all of which I knew to be well organized in the stock room. John suggested that I get my desk outfitted and then come in to see him. I was so anxious to actually get to work that ·I left most of the supplies in their bags and shoved them into the desk drawers. Five minutes later, I was standing in front of John's office; he was on the phone but motioned for me to come in and sit down. I sat and waited, and waited. I picked up a book on his coffee table and started reading. He kept holding up his forefinger and gesturing, "One more minute." Thirty minutes later he wrapped up the call and said, "Time for lunch. Come on, I'm buying." I smiled at Sherry as I walked by the board and signed "Out."

While at lunch, I was able to direct the conversation away from college basketball long enough to get some direction regarding my "work." (It would prove to be the most focused and informative meeting of my short tenure.) My first and most important responsibility was to validate the assessment instrument that served as the core business product of the business. The instrument was marketed as a personality and behavioral assessment that could predict employee performance and was being used by several Fortune 500 companies to make hiring, promotion, and placement decisions.

The instrument had been purchased several years earlier from a psychologist who assured Mary and John that it was valid and reliable, although he did not provide any documentation. I took the test, read the computer-generated report, and sensed immediately that it was a bad instrument. With the raw data of several thousand completed reports, it did not take me long to confirm my suspicion. The instrument failed even the most basic tests of reliability and validity. In fact, some of the scales and the manner in which they were scored made no sense at all. Had I still been teaching statistics and survey development, this would have served as an ideal example of what not to do. The report, which was generated and used to make decisions about people's careers, had all of the validity of a fortune cookie.

I explained my findings to Mary and John as straightfor- wardly as possible and let them know that they needed to immediately stop using the instrument. Put simply, they were committing fraud. John and Mary listened without comment and then asked me to step outside the door. After a few minutes Mary called me back in and said, "I think that pulling the instru- ment would confuse our clients." I was speechless. Mary asked if I could revise it—she liked this idea because they could then market it as a new and improved version. I told her that it might be possible to create a similar-*looking* instrument but that the majority of existing items would have to be thrown out. I also told her that the development and validation process would take several months.

I spent the next six weeks creating, testing, editing, and retesting items. After a dozen different versions I met with John and Mary to let them know that we were ready to begin the pilot study. As part of the research plan, four hundred employees from their largest client were to be surveyed. Mary praised me for a job well done and told me that plans had changed: there would be no pilot study. She had confidence in me and the new instrument. The marketing person was already working on a press release announcing the "New and Improved" version as immediately available. Speechless, I walked out.

I e-mailed John and Mary from home and apologized for my sudden departure. I reminded them of the importance of following the research plan and asked them to reconsider their decision. No response. The next morning I arrived at work early and typed my resignation letter. As soon as John arrived, I asked if he and Mary had reconsidered. He said that they really appreciated my hard work and were happy with the instrument as it was. I told him that I was glad they were happy but that wasn't a substitute for empirical research and handed him my resignation. I collected my things, watered the plants, wished them good luck, and slid my circle to "Out."

Birth of the RESPECT Model

Shortly after this experience, I was asked to give a two-hour presentation to an international group of plant managers on motivating employees in the twenty-first century. I knew a lot about motivation—it had been the topic of my doctoral dissertation. My initial plan was to review in detail fifteen different theories of motivation. Fortunately, I realized that not only would I put my audience to sleep but, more important, my talk was strictly academic and would be of little practical value. My goal became to deliver a message that would make a difference. I decided to start by identifying the most common factors among the models. After three months of drawing arrows and combining and recombining words on a giant whiteboard, only one factor remained: respect.

I realized that the concept of respect perfectly explained how in the span of two months I had gone from enthusiastic new hire to handing in my resignation. I had lost respect for the leaders of the organization and felt completely disrespected by their treatment of me and my work. I then began to think about all the jobs that I had held and realized that the more I felt respected and respected the organization, its leaders, my team members, and the work that I did, the more motivated I was. It was clear to me that respect was the lynchpin of employee motivation.

During this time, a friend introduced me to the concept of employee engagement. As I began to read about engagement, it became clear to me that successful organizations did not motivate employees; they engaged them. Traditional reward and recognition programs failed to increase productivity not because they failed to motivate people but because motivating people wasn't what mattered! What mattered was having committed employees who exhibited high levels of discretionary effort in support of the mission and vision of the organization. Theories of motivation were helpful in explaining bursts of energy in pursuit of a "carrot" but could not explain employee engagement. Motivating employees and engaging them were very distinct concepts.

I also realized that it was not so much that I had become unmotivated in my story but that I had become disengaged. I had gone from caring greatly to not caring at all, and I realized that it was still all about respect. In my life when I had been most dedicated to my work it was because I respected the work, the organization, and its people and felt respected in return. When I felt disrespected or lost respect for the organization and people, I disengaged, not only in my professional life but also in my personal life. The more I respected someone, the more I was drawn to him or her; the less I respected someone, the further removed I became physically and psychologically. The RESPECT Model was born.

The core of the RESPECT Model took about two years to develop and was based on considerable research, both my own and others'. The key was to determine the factors that affected people's experience of respect in the workplace. In the end, I identified seven factors that form the acronym RESPECT: Recognition, Empowerment, Supportive Feedback, Partnering, Expectations, Consideration, and Trust. Each of these contributes significantly to employees' feelings of respect and their level of engagement. Moreover, each factor can be positively affected by applying the principles of the RESPECT Model.

Over the years, I've worked with many organizations and seen the power of the RESPECT Model in practice. I've seen it transform individual leaders, teams, and entire organizations. The purpose of this book is to provide you with the resources and tools you need to implement the RESPECT Model in your organization. The book begins by distinguishing between employee motivation and engagement and goes on to discuss twenty reasons why traditional "carrot and stick" programs just don't work. You'll read about the concept of employee engagement, why it is so important, and why, unfortunately, much of the research is fundamentally flawed. Then you'll learn about the RESPECT Model and how it changes organizational culture and increases employee engagement. Each of the RESPECT drivers will be presented in its own chapter and will include specific examples and turnkey strategies to immediately begin increasing RESPECT in your organization. Trust, the last driver discussed, serves as a building block for all other drivers. If you already know that trust is an issue for you personally or in your organization, it is recommended that you read about this driver before the others. The last chapter provides useful suggestions on implementing the model and addresses the general decline of respect in society and its impact on the next generation of employees.

My hope is that this book remains within your reach and that its pages become well marked with your own notes. My intention is for you to bring the words on these pages to life so that you may foster a culture of RESPECT and engage the hearts and minds of your employees. This is not a book to be read—it is a book to be lived.

1

CHAPTER 1 # The Workplace "Carrot-on-a-Stick"

"The only carrots that interest me are the
number of carats in a diamond."

—*Mae West*

"Carrots and sticks" refers to using rewards and punishment to motivate others. This system is based on the principles of operant conditioning. Similarly, there is the expression "carrot-on-a-stick," which conjures up the image of a carrot tied to a stick held just beyond the reach of a donkey to encourage the animal to go faster. In organizations, "carrots" refer to rewards or incentives dangled in front of employees to motivate them to strive toward some goal. These incentives range from coffee mugs to lucrative financial bonuses and everything in between. The obvious assumption is that employees are actually motivated by the particular carrot being offered.

Operant Conditioning

Operant conditioning refers to specific behavioral strategies developed by B. F. Skinner to change behavior. Terms associated with Skinner's approach, such as *positive reinforcement*, *negative reinforcement*, and *punishment*, are often bantered about among human resources managers, business leaders, and consultants as they seek to motivate employees. Unfortunately, these terms have become widely misunderstood and misused.

Reinforcement—both positive and negative—refers to consequences that increase the likelihood of a behavior occurring in the future. Common forms of positive reinforcement include praise, privileges, money, and various rewards. Negative reinforcement refers to the removal of an aversive stimulus. For example, when a mother picks up a crying baby and the baby stops crying, the mother is negatively reinforced and thus more likely to pick up the baby when it cries in the future. Although it is possible to use negative reinforcement as a motivational strategy in the workplace, it is highly uncommon.

Punishment refers to adverse consequences that decrease the likelihood of the behavior occurring again in the future. Common forms of punishment include ignoring, penalties, fines, and taking away privileges. In the workplace, suspending an employee without pay is an example of using punishment to change behavior.

Here's the important part: in order for a consequence to be considered reinforcing or punishing, it must impact the probability of the behavior occurring again. If the consequence does not increase or decrease the likelihood of the behavior, then it does not meet the criteria as reinforcement or punishment.

This distinction is important because it suggests that whether a consequence is reinforcing or punishing depends on the individual and may differ further depending on the situation and source of the consequence (i.e., the person delivering it). For example, if your boss yells at you for being late to work and you start coming in on time, then the boss's yelling served as a form of punishment because it impacted your behavior. In contrast, if your wife yells at you for coming home late from work and your behavior does not change, then her yelling is not punishment—it is nagging.

It would be highly inaccurate and irresponsible of me to suggest that the principles of operant conditioning are ineffective. Thousands of empirical studies have demonstrated the power of operant conditioning to motivate animals, children, and adults to engage in specific behaviors in an effort to attain rewards. While in graduate school, I spent several years learning, researching, applying, and teaching these principles to help change the behavior of children diagnosed with conduct disorder. In fact, whether you realize it or not, we all use reinforcement and punishment every day in our personal lives. Whether you are feeding your cat because she is meowing for food, thanking your child for making his bed, or withholding affection from your significant other because he forgot your anniversary, you are using the techniques of operant conditioning to shape the behavior of those around you—as your behavior is being shaped in kind. I have always been frustrated by parents and supervisors who resist learning about the principles of behavior modification because they do not want to "manipulate" their children

There is no debate that operant conditioning can be used to motivate people to attain specific goals. The question is whether reward and recognition programs based on the principles of operant conditioning are effective and should be used in organizations. The answer is a resounding no.

or employees. You use these techniques every day; wouldn't it be nice to know what you're doing?

There is nothing wrong with the principles of operant conditioning. It is just that they don't work in the context of a business environment where you need people to use their minds. Fortunately, we don't have to worry about "fixing" traditional reward and recognition programs because the problem isn't with these programs at all; the problem is the fundamental, underlying assumption that to maximize the productivity of our employees we need to motivate them.

We have been led to believe that the same principles that get a mouse or pigeon to "work hard" are the ones that we should use to make human beings more productive. Here's the newsflash: human beings performing work in organizations are actually different from mice running in mazes and pressing bars for food pellets. People are complex beings filled with thoughts, feelings, attitudes, personalities, skills, experiences, and goals whose work is typically complex and requires higher-order cognitive skills including problem solving and decision making. Moreover, we work with other complex human beings in complex organizations. Although it may feel like it at times, we are not hamsters running on a wheel.

A Brief History of Human Motivation

For nearly all of human history, people have been motivated using "sticks," not "carrots." Why? Before the Industrial Revolution, there were few employees; most work that wasn't accomplished by the self-employed was done by slaves, criminals, and military personnel, and those who did not work hard were physically punished or killed, which are quite effective motivational techniques. It was not until the Industrial Revolution and the building of factories that there was a need to employ large numbers of free citizens. Thus, the roots of today's workforce are less than two hundred years old. (Pharaohs did not have to worry about the principles of operant conditioning!) In fact, it has been in only the past one hundred years that researchers, scientists, and business leaders have systematically approached the study of employee motivation and productivity. Let's take a look at some of the most important and influential work during this time.

Frederick Taylor—Father of Scientific Management

As factories and assembly lines grew, a new discipline emerged: scientific management. Often considered the father of this movement, Frederick Taylor published *The Principles of Scientific Management* in 1911. Taylor had worked for Bethlehem Steel and was interested in maximizing productivity. He undertook careful study of the tools, processes, and methods used in the manufacturing process. Coupled with the pioneering work of psychologists Frank and Lillian Gilbreth, time and motion studies became, and still are, a cornerstone of efficient manufacturing processes. Obvious but important, the work involved entirely manual labor and almost no thinking. In fact, referring to his studies with steel workers, Taylor wrote:

> *This work is so crude and elementary in its nature that the writer firmly believes that it would be possible to train an intelligent gorilla so as to become a more efficient pig-iron handler than any man can be. Yet it will be shown that the science of handling pig iron is so great and amounts to so much that it is impossible for the man who is best suited to this type of work to understand the principles of this science, or even to work in accordance with these principles without the aid of a man better educated than he is.*

Thus, the prevailing thinking was that thinking was not required. The focus was strictly on behavior and how to maximize an individual's output.

The Hawthorne Studies

Harvard Business School professor Elton Mayo was also concerned with the study and measurement of processes and environmental variables to increase employee productivity. Mayo and his colleagues worked with female employees who assembled telephone relays at Western Electric Hawthorne Works near Chicago from 1927 to 1932. During this time the researchers manipulated various factors such as light levels, work schedules, rest breaks, and refreshments. The women baffled the researchers by continuing to increase their productivity even under extremely unfavorable conditions, for example, very low levels of light. Mayo and his colleagues finally concluded that it was the attention given to these employees by the researchers that resulted in their increased performance; the finding became known as the Hawthorne Effect. Although there has been considerable controversy over this research and the conclusions drawn at the time, there is no question that it shed light on the importance of psychological factors affecting employee motivation and productivity, including worker autonomy, consulting with employees about their work, and paying attention to social factors in the workplace, including group cohesiveness and relations between supervisors and employees. If Taylor took away the "human" from the study of employee motivation and productivity, Mayo gave it back.

Skinner's Approach

The science of behavior was greatly furthered and forever changed by B. F. Skinner and his principles of operant conditioning introduced in *The Behavior of Organisms* (1938). Skinner used reinforcement and punishment techniques to motivate the behavior of lab animals such as mice and pigeons. These same principles and techniques proved to be highly effective in motivating human behavior and dovetailed perfectly with the field of scientific management and its focus on behavior. There appeared to be no need to consider people's thoughts or feelings to explain behavior. Thus, in what was becoming a tug-of-war of competing approaches to the study of motivation, Skinner succeeded in taking the "human" back out.

Henry Murray's Exploration in Personality

However, also published in 1938 and in stark contrast to Skinner, Henry Murray's book, *Explorations in Personality*, suggested that humans are motivated by factors such as their relationships to others and their level of professional achievement. Murray was the first psychologist to posit a theory of motivation based on such higher-order needs and would strongly influence David McClelland's Theory of Needs model. Murray recognized the importance of thoughts, feelings, and emotions as relevant to the study of human motivation. The tug-of-war continued.

Maslow's Hierarchy of Needs

In 1943, Abraham Maslow challenged Skinner's behaviorism model and suggested that a model of human motivation should be centered on people and not animals. Known as the father of humanistic psychology, Maslow's Hierarchy of Needs model explained human motivation based on meeting needs at different levels. At the lowest level were physiological needs such as food and water. At the second level were needs around safety and security. At level three, Maslow suggested that we seek to fulfill a sense of belonging and affiliation such as having friends and family and being part of a work group. Next, he hypothesized that we were driven by esteem issues such as achievement and respect. Finally, at level five, Maslow theorized that we seek personal growth and fulfillment.

Maslow's work has stood the test of time. In fact, his model readily predicts and explains human behavior during difficult economic times.

As people become more concerned about keeping their job, they are naturally going to be less focused on teamwork. Why? Because in teamwork one risks making others look good and not

When people begin to feel as though their jobs may be threatened and hence their security, they are much less concerned about their need for achievement or affiliation. That is why, in a down economy, team functioning breaks down.

getting full credit for one's accomplishments. People are less likely to share information, cooperate, or display discretionary effort unless doing so directly increases their perceived value to the organization. Breakdown in teamwork is well explained by Maslow's model. If you want people to function more cohesively as a team, they must feel secure in their jobs.

Since the 1950s there have been a number of significant developments in the field of human motivation and a plethora of theories to explain and impact human behavior in the workplace, including Albert Bandura's Self-Efficacy Theory, Douglas McGregor's Theory X and Theory Y, Victor Vroom's Expectancy Theory, Frederick Herzberg's Two-Factor Theory, Martin Fishbein's Expectancy-Value Theory, Edwin Locke's Goal-Setting Theory, and John Adams's Equity Theory. Each of these has contributed significantly to our understanding of employee motivation and productivity in the workplace. Collectively, this body of research provides overwhelming evidence that employees are motivated by their thoughts, feelings, and beliefs and that what was effective at motivating Skinner's lab animals to work for food pellets is too simplistic to fully explain the complexities of human motivation. Skinner lost the empirical tug-of-war. Given all this, it is difficult to understand why our primary approach to motivating employees continues to be reward and recognition programs based on the principles of operant conditioning. It just doesn't make sense.

Motivation in the Workplace Today

The workplace and its employees are very different today than they were prior to the second half of the twentieth century. One of the biggest changes is employees' expectations and their relationship to their work. Managers, leaders, and human resources professionals must be willing to give up traditional beliefs about the role of motivation and factors that affect employee motivation if they are to deal effectively with today's workforce.

Do Your Employees Enjoy Their Jobs?

The question of whether a person enjoyed his or her work is a recent and primarily Western phenomenon. Certainly through the 1950s, work served the primary purpose of putting food on the table and a roof over one's head. While people undoubtedly developed friendships at work and may even have enjoyed their work depending on their profession and position, such issues were not viewed as particularly relevant to making a living. Over the past few decades, employees have placed more and more importance on deriving a certain level of satisfaction and meaning from their work. This is particularly true once employees reach a certain monetary threshold that comfortably provides for their quality of life. Today's leaders who wish to maximize the productivity of their employees must fully understand and embrace the notion that employees work for more than just money; they work to feel good about themselves.

Show Me the Money!

Money can motivate individual performance; however, the impact on performance is typically short-lived. Money falls under what Frederick Herzberg called a Hygiene factor, in other words, a factor that has more to do with decreasing motivation than increasing it. Money matters a lot under two conditions. First, it matters at the very low end of the pay scale where an additional dollar an hour can make a significant difference to an individual. Second, it matters when people find out that they are being undercompensated relative to a colleague or market value;

this situation violates Equity Theory. A classic example occurs when a new employee is hired at a higher salary than an existing employee doing the same job. Under these conditions, the existing employee, who may have been perfectly satisfied with his pay, naturally becomes upset and feels unappreciated. Typically, the employee will quit, demand more money, or perform markedly worse. If an organization is going to hire a new employee with similar skills and education to an existing employee at a higher pay rate, my suggestion is to give an "equity raise" to your existing employee *before* the new employee comes aboard.

But I Know Motivation Works!

If we are talking about changing behavior, motivation techniques can be very helpful in raising a person's level of readiness to change and in getting him or her to begin engaging in desired behaviors. However, motivation is rarely enough to sustain behavior change over time. In the words of Jim Ryun, "Motivation is what gets you started; habits are what keep you going." I've been a group fitness instructor for almost a decade, have designed an organizational health and wellness program, have taught classes on behavior modification, and have done individual counseling with people to help them break poor habits and create healthy ones. I can tell you with certainty that nearly everyone who begins a diet or exercise program does so with great motivation, but if that initial inspiration is not supplemented with factors such as social support, education, and a sound exercise and nutrition program, most people will find themselves back where they started in just a few weeks. Similarly, many programs that try to motivate employees begin with a bang and fizzle out quickly. *Behaviors that change quickly also change back quickly.*

I would ask you to consider when is the last time that you were *really* motivated to change a behavior? Perhaps you wanted to get into great shape for a special occasion, such as getting married or going to a twenty-fifth high school reunion—both of which I did while writing this book. Maybe you had a physical and your doctor told you that you needed to stop smoking and lose weight. Notice first that it usually takes something really big in our lives to get us motivated to change our behavior. Second, it requires making a conscious choice to change our behavior and the habits that run our lives. Third, notice how even powerful events and conscious choices rarely lead to sustained changes in behavior. Habits are persistent and resistant to change, and they don't go away just because we feel suddenly motivated.

Being motivated rarely changes anyone's behavior over the long term. How many people do you know who have said they *really* want to stop drinking or smoking, start exercising, study a foreign language, learn to play an instrument, go back to school, get out of a bad relationship, or find a better job and have actually done so? By the way, when you hear someone saying that they are "trying" to do these things, it is *always* a sign that they have already decided to fail. I am suggesting that almost no source of motivation, even the promise of having someone say, "Wow, I can't believe how great you look after twenty-five years!" will provide enough incentive to keep you motivated for more than a few weeks. If it were, there would be a lot more people at reunions. Motivation may get you started down a path, but carrots alone are simply insufficient to develop sustainable changes in behavior.

Changing Expectations in a Changing World

In addition to looking for fulfillment in one's work, today's employees expect and seek balance in their lives. In fact, they are being motivated by things other than what work offers. The old model involved employees sacrificing family time for work because such a sacrifice was viewed as supporting the family. Today, people are sacrificing their work for more family and personal time. Why the change? First, many people who grew up with parents who worked so much that they were rarely home simply don't want that for their children. Today's parents—especially men—want to be more involved in their children's lives beginning at birth. Second, for economic and environmental reasons, there has been a recent cultural shift away from wanting more "stuff." As a result, we don't need to work quite as hard to earn money. Third, people are more concerned about their physical and mental well-being and are making conscious decisions to work less and take better care of themselves. All in all, it is not simply about working hard and making money.

There is one other critical change in the workplace that has affected employees' motivations—The Deal has been broken. By The Deal I mean the idea that companies are loyal to their employees, and in return, employees are loyal to them. This is no longer the case. Corporate scandals, greedy executives, outsourcing, downsizing, and cuts in employee benefits have all fostered a sense of cynicism and distrust among workers who no longer feel a sense of loyalty to their organization. In truth, why should they? This decrease in loyalty has led to high rates of turnover as employees seek a "better deal" from whoever is offering it. Of course, this has resulted in great costs to organizations. Unless in a strong union environment that offers some assurances and security, employees simply aren't very motivated to stay with one organization over the long term.

In sum, our understanding of motivation and the factors that motivate employees have changed over time. The Greatest Generation is not the workforce of today, and organizations need to understand that the "new deal" is that there isn't any deal—employees will leave for a better opportunity without hesitation. Moreover, employees are more willing than ever to work and earn less if it means being able to spend more time with their families and lead a more balanced life.

In the next chapter we will examine traditional reward and recognition programs and see how effective they are at motivating today's employees.

CHAPTER 2 # Reward and Recognition Programs Don't Work

"Don't worry when you are not recognized,
but strive to be worthy of recognition."

—*Abraham Lincoln*

Over the past several decades, organizations have spent literally billions of dollars creating and implementing reward and recognition programs in the hopes of motivating their employees and increasing morale. On the face of it, such an approach seems to make good sense; however, in terms of return on investment, the numbers just don't add up. In fact, most programs intended to motivate employees actually end up creating an overall deficit in employee motivation. While a handful of employees may be reinforced, many are left feeling punished. Programs that do elicit short-term benefits typically end up creating significant morale problems down the road. It's similar to retailers who advertise "zero down and no payments for six months." It sounds good now, but in the end it's going to cost you a whole lot more.

Although the evidence against the use of extrinsic rewards to motivate employees has been around for many years, business leaders and human resources professionals simply seem unwilling to accept it, perhaps because they don't know what else to do and the approach does seem sensible. My intention in this chapter is to put together such a comprehensive and compelling list of reasons against the use of traditional reward and recognition programs that their use can no longer be justified.

Tube Socks for Everyone

Several years ago I was hired by a large manufacturing company to help with its employee recognition and rewards program. In general, the company leaders wanted to motivate their employees and, specifically, to increase employees' compliance with safety requirements such as wearing hard hats, using eye and ear protection, and wearing seatbelts when operating a forklift. During my first visit I met with Tim, a senior member of the human resources department and the individual responsible for this initiative. While giving me a tour of the facility, he pointed out numerous employees violating safety procedures. When we got back to his office he began telling me how the company had tried "everything" to get employees to work safely. Everything included providing extensive safety training, holding team meetings, hanging signs, making announcements over the loudspeaker, and offering various incentives for months with no lost-time accidents.

The company had also tried a number of different rewards. For example, at the end of the first accident-free month everyone in the plant received a small fan that plugged into a car's cigarette lighter. He told me that these were very much appreciated given how hot the summer months got in their part of the country. Unfortunately, one of the fans had been defective and caused an electrical short in an employee's car, causing the car to catch fire in the plant parking lot. Fortunately, no one was hurt. You can just imagine the headline in the local paper: "Car Burns Thanks to Safety Recognition Program."

After this event, they decided to avoid electrical incentives and stick with traditional giveaways such as logo-embossed T-shirts, hats, and coffee mugs. Tim said that employees did not seem very excited by these prizes. No kidding. However, in the past few months, they had come upon a reward that was receiving a very favorable response—a three-pack of tube socks. The previous month, employees had lined up to get their socks. Tim was concerned, however, that the incentive program was working too well. There were rumors that employees and supervisors were covering up minor accidents so as not to ruin it for everyone in the plant. For example, one employee was mysteriously sent home early only to return the next day with several stitches on his forearm supposedly from changing a tire on his car. Another fellow spent most of the shift in the break room with a bag of ice on his head for a sudden headache while others covered for him. You see this kind of team support for guys with headaches all the time, right?

On the one hand, Tim was pleased by the power of the tube sock program and by the apparent uptick in employee camaraderie. Certainly, three months with zero lost-time accidents made him and the human resources department look good. The plant manager was happy. Corporate was happy. At the same time, Tim was concerned that someone might get seriously hurt and it wouldn't be reported. He asked if I had any thoughts on how they might tweak the program. Where should I begin?

"Tim," I said, "creating a 'program' sends the message that working safely is optional—and I don't think that is what you want to communicate. What if you walked up to one of your noncompliant forklift drivers and said, 'The number one priority for this company is the safety of its employees. We want every employee to return safely to his or her family at the end of every day. In an effort to make sure that happens, we have specific policies and procedures that you have chosen to ignore. I am sending you home for the rest of the day and giving you two more days off without pay. I would request that you use this time to think about whether you can work for a company that cares about your well-being and comply with the safety guidelines.'"

Tim replied, "Yeah, but the guys really seem to like the tube socks. I'm afraid a lot of employees will get upset if we get rid of the program." As a consultant, I've found there are times when remaining professional requires biting down so hard on one's bottom lip that you risk breaking skin. This was one of those times. Of course, if I did start bleeding, I was pretty sure that Tim would be willing to look the other way. "Tim, I've got an idea. At the beginning of every month, put a big barrel of socks outside your office and let whoever would like some come by and pick them up." "But then the program won't mean much, will it?" I felt a drop of blood.

Twenty Reasons Why Reward and Recognition Programs Don't Work

Many of the points that follow are illustrated using examples from my work with clients. I want to be clear that in every case the sponsors of these programs were well-meaning, caring people doing their best to improve their organizations—just like

Tim. It is not my intention to insult or embarrass them or anyone else using such programs. My only goal is to educate and help you understand why recognition programs fail.

Reason 1: Programs Fail Because They Are Programs

Reward and recognition programs fail for the same reason that diets fail—because they are *programs*! Programs are nearly always designed to accomplish a specific goal in a relatively short time period, for example, losing weight for a college reunion. Here's a great illustration of the difference between the short-term impact of a program and the longer-term impact of changing one's lifestyle. My friend Mary tries every new diet that comes out, and she is constantly losing and gaining the same fifty pounds. Recently, I saw her and she looked great. I said, "Wow, what diet are you on?" She responded, "I'm not on a diet." That is the right answer! Programs fail because people view them as something to be done for a period of time and not as something that needs to be incorporated into their lifestyle. If you're a healthy person, you eat healthy food—not because you are *trying* to lose weight or be healthy, but because who you are is a healthy person and healthy people take care of themselves. Can you develop programs that create "yo-yo" motivated employees? Yes, but is that what you want? No, what you want are employees who work hard all the time and not just when they are chasing carrots.

> Programs don't fundamentally change employees' beliefs or commitment to their job; they just change their behavior during the course of the program.

Employees are motivated to work toward the goal only as long as the program continues. You don't see many people continuing to run once they have crossed the finish line. When one person yells "Bingo" the game is pretty much over. Presumably, you don't want employees to be motivated only when programs are in place. If an organization is not careful, it will condition its employees to do just that—the way retail stores have conditioned people to shop only during sales. It should not be about temporary bursts of energy; it should be about continuous improvement based on the belief that getting better or working hard matters for its own sake and not for some external reward.

Reason 2: Rewards Are Not Necessarily Reinforcing

The most basic assumption of reward and recognition programs is that the "donkey" wants the carrot. I grew up on a farm with horses and donkeys. This may surprise you, but not all donkeys like carrots. Organizations always assume they know what employees will find desirable.

For example, a company might offer an extra vacation day as an incentive; in some companies many employees do not use all their vacation—especially in the United States. Why work for something you're not going to use? A friend works at a company where they give gas cards to the employee of the month. Last month it went to the security guard who doesn't own a car. In some cases the supposed reward can actually result in employees

> Even those rewards that might appear to be most obviously desirable do not necessarily work for everybody.

purposely putting in less effort so as not to be recognized! This commonly occurs in monthly programs where the same person wins each month and ends up becoming embarrassed. I have also seen it occur in peer pressure situations where winning would be viewed as "playing management's game." And, if winning might result in a promotion—guess what?—many employees consider being promoted undesirable, especially if it requires giving up overtime hours or having to move to another location. So, rewards aren't always rewarding.

Reason 3: Programs Are Too Narrowly Focused

Programs tend to be narrowly focused on a specific goal, such as production or sales numbers, which often leads to ignoring other important aspects of one's work. In fact, programs that focus on a single target goal can actually be deleterious. For example, individually rewarding salespeople for "hitting their numbers" may pit employees against one another and hamper teamwork, trust, and customer service. When production is the goal, safety and quality often suffer. As an analogy, imagine going to the gym and for one month exclusively working your biceps. In terms of overall health, is that really as smart as spending your time in a more balanced workout routine? This is not to say that one doesn't look to focus on areas of opportunity, but physical and organizational health does not come from a focus on just one area.

Reason 4: Programs Focus on the Wrong Dependent Variable

Programs nearly always focus on a single outcome measure instead of focusing on the processes that would result in accomplishing the goal. As an analogy, basketball teams focus on fundamentals and conditioning because doing so leads to scoring baskets and winning games. Reward and recognition programs focus on scoring baskets and ignore the fundamentals, like communication, teamwork, training, and other important tools needed to "win" over time. Focus on improving your organization's fundamentals, and I promise you will score more baskets.

Reason 5: Goals Can Limit Performance

Although setting goals is an important part of any performance management system, they should be viewed as stepping-stones and opportunities to celebrate improvement and successes, not as finish lines. Mike Krzyzewski, Duke University's men's basketball coach, authored what I consider to be the best hands-on leadership book ever written—*Leading from the HEART*. It should be required reading for every leader in your organization. Among my favorite quotes is: "I never have a goal that involves number of wins—never. It would just tend to limit our potential." By their nature, goals suggest an upper limit and create an artificial ceiling. The focus should be on working hard in all aspects of the game—if that is the approach, you win games as a natural consequence.

Reason 6: Inconsistent and Unfair Administration

If you want to spark a passionate conversation at your organization, tell supervisors that you are beginning an employee reward and recognition program. Invariably, you will get the argument, "Why should we reward our employees for doing their jobs? Isn't that why they get a paycheck?!" They have a point. Supervisors, the usual gatekeepers of such programs, vary widely in their beliefs about such efforts and subsequently in their support of them. Some supervisors refuse to play at all and mock the program.

Perceptions of inequity among employees are *impossible* to prevent. Even when program guidelines are clear and supervisors willingly adhere to them, employees will complain of favoritism within and across teams. In reality, supervisors simply cannot help but have biased perceptions of employees that result in conscious or unconscious favoritism. As such, some employees are going to malign the program as "unfair" and often are able to point to ready examples of inconsistent administration that support their view. These tend to be the lowest-performing employees. Depending on how loud their voice grows, their complaints can seriously undermine the program and cause considerable stress for supervisors.

Beyond the impact of these attitudinal differences, some supervisors have limited opportunity to observe the targeted behavior(s) due to work schedules, physical proximity, and simply being overwhelmed with their "real" work. Another factor that contributes to inconsistent and unfair distribution of rewards is having a fair playing field. For example, imagine a sales incentive program that gives a bonus for those with sales over "X" amount for a given month. Typically, more senior salespeople have advantages such as better sales territories, product lines, or even hours at their retail stores. Junior salespeople begin with such a clear disadvantage that it is unlikely they will even bother to participate. Goals have to be challenging but reachable.

You may be thinking that one obvious remedy is to base the program on a percentage increase. For example, any salesperson who increases his or her own average sales over the past three months by 10 percent will win the reward. Now you give the advantage to your poorest performers who have the greatest

> One of the major reasons that reward and recognition programs are unfairly administered is that the program guidelines are unclear and open to interpretation.

room for improvement. It will be far more difficult for your hardest-working, most productive salespeople to increase their sales by 10 percent. Do you really want to punish your best salespeople and reward your poorest performers for actually stepping up one month? I didn't think so.

Exactly what does being a good team player or dealing effectively with a difficult customer look like? This kind of ambiguity will result in supervisors interpreting the program criteria differently and lead to inconsistent administration, which in turn will lead to more ammunition for disgruntled employees who view the program as biased and unfair. Unfortunately, it is nearly impossible to create a program that provides an equal playing field for all employees. In sum, try as you might, you will never create a program that is and appears to be fair to everyone.

Reason 7: Added Stress for Supervisors

First-line supervisors who are typically responsible for the administration of reward and recognition programs are among the most stressed individuals in any organization. The responsibilities associated with these programs increase their already burdensome workload. Moreover, they often create considerable stress for supervisors who don't want to be put in a position of being accused of playing favorites or having employees "sucking up" just to earn recognition. In response, many give points out to everyone regardless of performance in an effort to appear fair. Of course, such an approach is totally unfair to the top performers and causes their morale to decrease. Do you really want a program that adds more stress to your supervisors and takes them away from their primary job of increasing employee productivity? Ironic, isn't it?

Reason 8: Programs Foster Cheating

My father always told me, "Don't make people into cheaters." Growing up, I never quite knew what this meant, but I finally do: Don't create circumstances under which good people will be tempted to break the rules. Unfortunately, this is a frequent issue with reward and recognition programs. Just look at the tube socks example. Supervisors and employees violated serious safety procedures for the sake of winning socks!

Cheating or deception of some form tends to occur in most programs. Examples range from the fairly benign to the illegal, including expediting or delaying orders or expenses, withholding information or providing misleading information, taking shortcuts, stealing customers, or in some other way attempting to make oneself look better than one's fellow co-workers. Programs with high-value rewards and few winners are most likely to turn employees into cheaters.

Pharmaceutical companies are famous for holding sales contests in which representatives can earn large bonuses and elaborate vacations. As you probably know, the pharmaceutical industry has been heavily regulated in an effort to prevent sales representatives from more or less bribing doctors into writing prescriptions for their products. So, the days of luxury golf outings have been commonly replaced with "take-in" lunch for the office staff. Meet Linda—a thirty-five-year-old pharmaceutical sales representative from New Jersey. She has a personal credit card and an arrangement with an upscale restaurant in her territory. All of her "docs" are welcome to enjoy dining with family and friends on her dime at any time. In fact, one doctor recently threw a sweet sixteen birthday party at the restaurant for his daughter and let Linda pick up the four-figure tab.

Are all sales representatives so unscrupulous? Of course not. Do reward and recognition programs cause all employees to cheat the system? No. However, the larger the reward, the more likely it is that people are going to look for ways to bend rules and work around the system to gain an advantage. I recognize that these programs are created with the best of intentions in mind, but their very nature can promote unwanted, unethical, unscrupulous, and sometimes illegal behavior. I don't think you want programs that turn your employees into cheaters.

Reason 9: Programs Destroy Teamwork

I don't mean to pick on salespeople, but corporate incentive programs often put this population at greatest risk for cheating and creating significant collateral damage to team members and the organization as a whole. This is particularly true when employees are compensated largely on individual commissions. In such circumstances, team members are often viewed as competitors. Car dealerships are well known for creating cutthroat environments and monthly programs that reward the top salespeople. Invariably, such programs foster unhealthy competition and undermine teamwork, which often comes across as unprofessional to customers.

You may have already jumped to the solution of team-based programs. In addition to the problems raised with the tube socks examples, there are others. Within any team you are going to have employees with different skill levels, commitment to the organization, and interest in the carrot. Team members also differ in their commitments and responsibilities outside of work, such as school-aged children, which limit their ability to exert additional discretionary effort outside of normal business hours. These factors result in some employees having the desire and

> Whether individual or team-based, reward and recognition programs almost always hurt teamwork.

ability to increase their productivity, others having little interest or ability to contribute, and the rest somewhere in between. Invariably, the hardworking, motivated employee gets frustrated for "pulling the load." In the end, win or lose, the employees who were the most motivated will feel the most cheated.

Reason 10: Programs Are Cover-Ups for Ineffective Supervisors

We have established that reward and recognition programs are designed to motivate employees. Isn't that the job of the supervisor? Effective supervisors don't need—or want—programs to motivate their employees. Think about the most effective supervisors you've known; was any of their success due to running some sort of contest to motivate their employees? Organizations typically create reward and recognition programs in response to incompetent supervisors unable to motivate their people. So, even if a reward program did manage to motivate employees, it is only a short-term fix because you haven't addressed the underlying problem of the ineffective supervisor. Doesn't it make more sense to train and educate supervisors so that they have the skills to be successful in their jobs?

Reason 11: Programs Offer a Weak Reinforcement Schedule

There are several factors that increase the effectiveness or power of positive reinforcement. We have already covered the most obvious—the carrot actually being desired by the donkey.

Time between the occurrence of the behavior and delivery of the reward is another critical factor. Reinforcement is most powerful when it occurs immediately after the desired behavior. Imagine, for example, telling a donkey that he did a good job but he'll have to wait a few months before getting his carrot. In practice, there is often substantial lag time between behavior and reinforcer. People work harder to receive rewards that can be realized sooner rather than later. On a day-to-day basis, year-end rewards and employee-of-the-month programs do little to motivate behavior.

Nearly all reward and recognition programs follow the weakest possible schedule of reinforcement and the one most susceptible to extinction (*extinction* meaning that the behavior stops once the reward is no longer given). In strong reinforcement schedules, the behavior continues in the absence of the reinforcer for long periods of time. Consider for a moment the difference between the reinforcement schedules of a soda machine and a slot machine. Put a dollar in the soda machine and get a soda. Now, put a dollar in the soda machine and get nothing. How many more dollars do you put in before you stop? Notice how quickly the lack of reinforcement (getting your drink) extinguishes the behavior of putting your dollar in the machine. In contrast, people will put dollar after dollar in a slot machine without getting paid off. Technically speaking, slot machines work on what is called a variable ratio reinforcement schedule—you don't know how frequently you are going to win or how much. This schedule keeps people highly motivated. In contrast, soda machines and nearly all reward and recognition programs are based on a fixed schedule, which is considerably less motivating.

You may be thinking, "Why is he wasting my time writing about soda and slot machines?!" Well, if you're going to use reward and recognition programs, understanding the reinforcement schedules makes a big difference. Here is just one example. Fred had recently become the plant manager at a company where I did some consulting, and he very much wanted every employee to know the company mission statement by heart. He had big posters containing the mission statement plastered all over the plant and had wallet-sized laminated cards made for all employees, but they still didn't seem to get it. I had him call an "all-hands" meeting and announce the following: "Over the next month, I will be walking around the plant and randomly asking employees to recite the mission statement. If you get it correct, I will present you with five envelopes. Inside each envelope will be a cash amount: $5, $10, $20, $50, or $100. You get to pick the envelope and keep whatever is inside." Needless to say, everyone knew the mission statement by the end of the month.

I know it sounds like this was a successful program—and it was in the sense that it met the plant manager's expectations—but there are two fatal flaws. First, as soon as the program ends, people will inevitably start forgetting the statement, and within a few months most won't remember it. That's because programs work only while the reinforcer is available. Second, and more important, memorizing a mission statement is far different from living it. Getting employees to commit words to memory is a good first step. However, to have any real meaning, it needs to be followed up by a program reinforcing employee behavior consistent with the mission statement. Of course, such a program would suffer from many of the problems we have identified and will continue to identify. Putting aside the mission statement example, the key takeaway is simply that most reward and recognition programs are designed with the weakest possible reinforcement schedule and the one most susceptible to extinction.

Reason 12: Giving Gifts Is Not a Reinforcement Program

Sherry was the part-time human resources manager for a computer start-up company with about thirty employees. Joe, the company CEO, shared that he was concerned about company morale and asked if she had any ideas. She knew about positive reinforcement and decided to surprise the employees by handing out twenty-dollar gift certificates for the movies on a Friday afternoon. The employees loved it—what a nice surprise! The following Monday she and the CEO could see how much more enthusiastic people appeared and decided to hand out gift cards to a chain restaurant with the paychecks that Friday. The employees were visibly appreciative, but come Monday they did not seem as motivated as the prior Monday. That Friday she left twenty-dollar gas cards on people's desks.

Joe was a friend of mine and told me about their gift card program. While he liked doing nice things for employees, he was beginning to doubt whether it really was having any impact, and they had already spent $1,800 in three weeks. I met with Sherry, who shared that she was confused and concerned because the program seemed to be losing its impact. After three weeks, employees were not noticeably more enthusiastic than when the program began. She was also quite taken aback when two employees stopped by her cubicle to ask for their gift on Thursday because they would not be around on Friday. Moreover, some of the salespeople in the field who had heard about this program complained because they were being left out.

I explained that she had not created a reward and recognition program; she had created an entitlement program. When a reward is not contingent upon a behavior, it is a gift—not a reinforcer. Gifts are nice, but they have very little impact on behavior. Unfortunately, many reward and recognition initiatives have morphed into entitlement programs. Although such programs aren't motivating anyone, removing the program is likely to cause a decrease in morale. Employees get upset when they don't get what they feel they deserve—even if they didn't do anything to earn it. Depending on how long the program has been in place and how much it costs, you may just want to leave it intact—let people have their tube socks. Bottom line, if you're going to create such a program, make sure the reward is contingent on performance.

Reason 13: Programs Reduce Creativity and Risk Taking

When it comes to the possibility of winning a reward, most people are risk-averse. They don't want to risk losing because they tried some new, clever approach that did not pan out. Traditional reward and recognition programs reinforce doing it by the book—not experimentation. Thus, employees go with tried and true approaches that have worked in the past. Such programs may get people to work harder but discourage innovation, creativity, and risk taking—the very behaviors that actually make a long-term difference in your organization.

Reason 14: Extrinsic Reinforcement Reduces Intrinsic Motivation

Research dating back nearly forty years to the work of social psychologist Edward Deci demonstrates that one's intrinsic motivation for a task decreases when it is reinforced with a material reward such as money. Intrinsic motivation refers to activities that people find rewarding on their own. For most people, these are best exemplified by hobbies such as playing a musical instrument, reading, writing poetry, and gardening. While some people might find pulling weeds a chore, others enjoy it immensely. Just like extrinsic motivation, intrinsic motivation depends on the individual.

Obviously, jobs are not hobbies and employees get paid; however, the more emphasis put on the extrinsic reward, the less internal motivation an employee feels toward the task. Reward and recognition programs actually diminish the perceived value of the task to the employee; psychologically the employee is doing the task not because it is important but because he or she can benefit from it materially. The more an employee values the task, the more he or she will see it as personally rewarding and be internally motivated, which explains why people who work for nonprofit agencies generally report much higher levels of job satisfaction than those employed by for-profit organizations, even though those at the for-profits make considerably more money. Supervisors would be wise to spend more time helping their employees see the value and importance of their work.

Reason 15: Wrong Behaviors Are Rewarded

Many reward programs not only fail to reinforce the intended behavior but also inadvertently reinforce the behavior they are meant to discourage! As Steven Kerr wrote in his classic 1975 *Academy of Management Journal* article, "On the Folly of Rewarding A, While Hoping for B," "Numerous examples exist of reward systems that are fouled up in that behaviors which are rewarded are those which the one doing the rewarding is trying to *discourage*, while the behavior he desires is not being rewarded at all."

For example, organizational leaders may speak of the importance of teamwork but then create programs that recognize and reinforce individual performance. This may well result in rewarding the individual who is the *least* team player. I recommend that you examine your reward and incentive programs to ensure that you are not accidentally reinforcing behaviors that run counter to the values of your organization.

Reason 16: Everybody's a Winner

In Lewis Carroll's *Alice in Wonderland,* the DoDo announced: "Everybody has won, and all must have prizes." Sometimes organizations create reward programs in which the bar is set so low that nearly everyone wins. Such programs fail to distinguish productive, hardworking employees from those who just show up, which results in reducing the morale of the best employees, who feel that the program devalues their efforts. The message is: "Any level of performance is great!" Review the criteria of any current programs and make sure that the bar is set appropriately.

Reason 17: Programs Are Manipulative

Some employees view motivation programs for what they are—manipulation. In fact, your best employees are those most likely to be offended by such programs. Just as some supervisors say, "Why should I recognize employees for doing their job?" some employees will say, "I don't need some award to tell me that I've done a good job." Such people take pride in their job and work ethic and feel babied by getting acknowledged for doing what they get paid to do. Top performers also recognize that these programs are often intended to motivate those who are not working hard and are often frustrated that resources are being spent on their underperforming team members. If you want to motivate your top performers, hold those who are not doing their job accountable.

Reason 18: Program Architects Are Generally Not Experts

Human resources managers and associates, the primary architects of these programs, are, quite frankly, rarely qualified to create them. Having taken a few psychology classes in college does not make one an expert in the theories of motivation and how to practically apply their principles in the workplace. In fact, most human resources managers that I've met think that negative reinforcement is some form of punishment. If they misunderstand such basic terms, how can they possibly create an effective program?

In fairness, especially in a smaller company, most human resources managers are generalists who are required to have knowledge in many, many areas and should not be expected to have such expertise. At the same time, such professionals should take responsibility for knowing what they don't know and not take on projects for which they are unqualified, because, as we have seen, they often cause more harm than good. If you are intent on developing motivation programs, I encourage you to seek the guidance of a qualified behavioral psychologist.

Reason 19: Programs Have No Impact on Workplace Culture

Reward and recognition programs will never lead to long-term, sustainable changes in behavior because they have no impact on organizational culture. This is the fundamental reason why these programs should be dismissed. *Culture drives behavior, and behavior reinforces culture.* When you take a new job you either fit into the culture, acclimate to fit the culture, or leave. The behaviors of incumbent employees serve to inculcate new employees into the culture of the organization. We are social beings extremely sensitive to fitting in and take our cues from those around us. In fact, our desire to conform is so strong that we will actually disregard what we know to be true in order to avoid being the odd man out. Whether it is your place of work or worship, a social club, or a health club, there is an associated culture that tells you how to act and even what to believe.

How many times have you heard, "That is just the culture around here"? "That" may refer to anything from showing up late to meetings to not returning phone calls to pointing fingers to cutting corners. Think back on the last time you took a new job. One of the first things you did consciously or unconsciously was to figure out "how things work." You watched and paid attention to the behavior of others. Do people tend to come in early and work late? Do people eat lunch at their desks? How do people act around the boss? Do people chat much about personal issues during work? Do people check their Blackberrys during meetings? Do people bring work home at night? Do people hang out together outside of work? How do people keep their desks? How do people dress? These and countless other questions go through our minds as we figure out how to adjust our behaviors to fit in.

Some organizations are famous for their culture, with Google's emphasis on having fun, being creative, constant innovation, teamwork, and open communication being a prime example. Strong cultures are built around an organization's mission, vision, and core values established by the founders. The stronger the culture, the more consistent it remains over time and the greater its impact on each employee's behavior. How do reward and recognition programs influence culture? They don't. As soon as the program is over, any changes in behavior will fail to be reinforced and quite possibly will be punished by the social mores of the organization. If you want to achieve meaningful and long-term changes in behavior, you have to impact the culture, and you simply can't do that with any kind of program.

Reason 20: Reward Programs Decrease Overall Motivation

I have saved the strongest point for last. Most agree that the purpose of reward and recognition programs is to increase the overall level of employee motivation. With this in mind, consider the following:

Question: Which employees are typically recognized by such programs?

Answer: The top performers in the organization.

Discussion: So, the most motivated and productive employees are the ones being acknowledged and reinforced by the programs. How much more motivated and productive can they be? This is like giving extra help to the student who makes a 98 percent on an exam. There isn't much room for improvement.

Question: What kind of impact do these programs have on the lowest-performing, least motivated employees?

Answer: Either none or negative.

Discussion: If only the top performers are going to get recognized, well, they aren't one of them. For the poor performers, such programs are simply reminders of how unappreciated they are and how disenfranchised they feel. At the absolute best, such programs will have no impact; more realistically, such employees will feel even less motivated.

Question: What impact will the program have on the majority of employees who fall between the very bottom and the very top?

Answer: Negative.

Discussion: During the program, many of these employees will increase their discretionary effort as they try for the "carrot." Psychologically, the employees who have increased their efforts and have not been recognized will become demoralized and adopt the attitude, "Why should

I bother working harder if I don't get anything for it?" The discretionary effort of these employees actually dips *below* what it was before the program.

In the end, while you may have minimally reinforced a few of your most motivated people, your program has had no impact on your poor performers and served to decrease the motivation of the middle employees, who represent the greatest potential to increase your overall human capital. I realize that this may be difficult to accept, but it's true: traditional reward and recognition programs that seek to motivate employees actually do more harm than good.

Leaving Your Reward and Recognition Programs Behind

To summarize, traditional recognition and reward programs based on the principles of operant conditioning are doomed before they commence. Under the best of circumstances, such programs are relatively benign and reinforce only those employees who are already the most engaged and productive. More likely they lead to breakdowns in team functioning, decrease creativity and risk taking, create stress for supervisors, and decrease the motivation of the very employees who present the greatest opportunity to increase your human capital. Thus, organizations spend valuable resources creating and administering programs that, at best, provide no return on their investment and are most likely to produce a negative one. If carrots don't work, what does?

CHAPTER 3 # Employee Engagement

> "There are three kinds of people: those who make things happen, those who watch things happen, and those who ask, 'What happened?'"
>
> —*Casey Stengel*

I hope you are now convinced that trying to motivate employees with "carrots" will not increase the overall human capital of your organization. How then do we create employees *who make things happen*? In this chapter, you will learn the important distinction between motivation and employee engagement, why you should stop trying to motivate employees altogether and focus on engaging them, the benefits of having an engaged workforce, and the factors that impact employee engagement. In addition, we will discuss current research findings as well as the widespread misunderstanding and invalid measurement of engagement. Let's begin by clearly defining employee engagement and distinguishing it from motivation.

What Is Employee Engagement?

I've given a lot of presentations over the years on the topic of employee engagement. The one that I remember best occurred a few days after I proposed to my wife, Karen. While defining the concept of engagement for my audience it suddenly hit me: "I'm engaged!" I remembered what a life-changing commitment I was making and how dramatically different it felt from dating or even living together. Indeed, engagement is all about commitment; the word comes from the Old French (*en* + *gage*) meaning "to pledge oneself." Although not quite so life-altering, the concept of employee engagement is also about the extent to which one is committed, dedicated, and loyal to one's organization, supervisor, work, and colleagues. When you're truly committed, motivation becomes a lot less relevant—you're in it for the long haul.

How Is Employee Engagement Different from Employee Motivation?

Engagement is similar to, but not synonymous with, motivation. Engagement refers to an intrinsic, deep-rooted, and sweeping sense of commitment, pride, and loyalty that is not easily altered. In contrast, motivation level is strongly influenced by external factors, especially expectations that certain efforts or accomplishments will yield valued rewards, such as a financial bonus for meeting a quarterly sales objective.

Critically, a high level of engagement buffers the impact of negative environmental factors on motivation. In other words, highly engaged employees will remain motivated despite adverse circumstances, such as limited resources, equipment failures, time pressures, and so on. In contrast, employees with low levels of engagement will tend to appear motivated only under favorable conditions or when attempting to reach tangible, short-term goals that will yield personal reward. Motivated employees want to get through the work as quickly as possible to get to their carrots—regardless of what may be going on around them. In contrast, engaged employees keep their eyes on the goal but also use their peripheral vision to look for opportunities that may contribute further to accomplishing the mission of the organization. To reiterate, employees who are motivated but not engaged will work hard when there is something in it for them. Engaged employees work hard for the sake of the organization and because it gives them a feeling of fulfillment.

How Can I Tell the Difference Between a Motivated Employee and an Engaged Employee?

Imagine observing a team of employees frantically working to meet a deadline. If they meet the deadline, everyone receives a bonus. As you watch, everyone appears highly motivated—they are working hard to get to the carrot. Suddenly, there's an equipment failure that nearly ensures their inability to accomplish the goal. Now you have two groups of employees—those who say, "Oh well, we tried" and those who say, "What is it that we can still get accomplished?" The first group was motivated; the second group was engaged. *Engaged employees are hardy; motivated employees are opportunistic.* While motivation can wax and wane, engagement leads to a consistent level of performance.

The Profile of an Engaged Employee

While doing research on employee engagement, I surveyed individuals from more than one hundred organizations worldwide. Among the questions asked was: "How do you know if someone is engaged?" To really understand engagement in the workplace, I wanted to know the specific behaviors that characterized engaged employees. Such data is critical for developing a valid assessment instrument to measure engagement and interventions to increase it. As you might imagine, participants provided many different answers to the question. The following list contains the ten most frequent responses to the question of how you know an employee is engaged:

1. Brings new ideas to work
2. Is passionate and enthusiastic about work
3. Takes initiative
4. Actively seeks to improve self, others, and business
5. Consistently exceeds goals and expectations
6. Is curious and interested; asks questions
7. Encourages and supports team members
8. Is optimistic and positive; smiles
9. Overcomes obstacles and stays focused on tasks; is persistent
10. Is committed to the organization

In my opinion, the most complete response did not make our top-ten list: "They act as though they have ownership in the business." This statement reflects perfectly the attitude of highly engaged employees. Like the small business owner, such workers do whatever needs to be done, regardless of their job title. They come in early, leave late, and take work home if needed. They leave you e-mails and voice mails after work hours that begin, "I was just thinking . . ." They worry about the little things. If they see a piece of trash lying on the floor they pick it up—not because someone is watching but because they take great pride in their workplace. If there is a problem, they handle it; they don't ignore it or pass it down the line. They think about what they are doing and in the process come up with remarkable ideas to improve your business and satisfy your customers. They respectfully challenge you and their team members when they disagree. They treat the organization's money like it was their own. In sum, highly engaged employees do whatever they can to make the organization succeed.

You cannot buy engagement, and you certainly cannot demand it. I remember explaining the concept of engagement to a client who became very enthusiastic and said, "I want you to go tell my employees to get engaged!" It doesn't work that way. In truth, the extent to which employees are engaged has a lot less to do with them and a lot more to do with their supervisor and the organization as a whole. Not every employee is going to think and behave as a business owner would. However, by the end of this book, you will learn how to work with your employees so they understand and incorporate this "business owner" perspective more fully into their own work. With that in mind, how engaged are your employees?

EMPLOYEE ENGAGEMENT ASSESSMENT QUIZ

Read each statement below and decide how accurately it describes your employees using the following scale:

- **a. Never or rarely engage in this behavior (0 points)**
- **b. Sometimes engage in this behavior (1 point)**
- **c. Regularly engage in this behavior (2 points)**
- **d. Always or almost always engage in this behavior (3 points)**

Place the point value of your answer choice on the blank line next to the statement.

_____ 1. **Employees appear passionate about their work.**

_____ 2. **Employees speak with pride about the organization.**

_____ 3. **Employees demonstrate high levels of discretionary effort.**

_____ 4. **Employees take the initiative to correct mistakes, even if it was outside the scope of their normal responsibilities.**

_____ 5. **Employees regularly offer specific suggestions for improvement.**

_____ **Total Number of Points**

INTERPRETING YOUR SCORES

0-5: You have a significant problem with employee engagement in your organization. Your employees are largely underperforming relative to their potential. Scores this low indicate that the problem is not limited to a few employees and disengagement has actually become the cultural norm of your organization.

6-10: Although there may be a moderate level of engagement across your workforce, it is more likely that some employees are engaged while others are disengaged. Overall, you may be getting only 50 percent of the discretionary effort that employees have to offer. That's leaving a lot of human capital on the table. Scores in this range are consistent with, at best, maintaining the status quo.

11-15: Congratulations, your score suggests a highly engaged workforce! The culture of your department or organization is one that fosters employee involvement, loyalty, and dedication. Employees are fully in the game and using high levels of discretionary effort to reach the goals and objectives of your organization. Your engaged workforce gives you a competitive advantage.

Regardless of your score on the quiz, the chapters that follow will help you increase and maintain high levels of engagement in your organization. Next, we look at reasons why having an engaged workforce contributes so substantially to organizational vitality.

Benefits of an Engaged Workforce

According to the consulting firm DDI, "The higher the level of engagement, the higher the performance of the business. The research is not inconclusive, not limited to one country or industry, and not contained to a few hundred people—it's overwhelming." There is no debate regarding the financial impact of employee engagement. Later in this chapter, we will examine findings from selected research studies. For now, I've listed the many factors that have been associated with higher levels of engagement:

- Increased productivity
- Increased profitability
- Higher-quality work
- Improved efficiency
- Lower turnover
- Reduced absenteeism

- Less employee theft and fraud
- Higher rates of customer satisfaction
- Higher employee satisfaction
- Reduced lost-time accidents
- Fewer Equal Employment Opportunity (EEO) complaints

Although, as we will discuss, methodological concerns temper these findings, the overall body of evidence strongly suggests that employee engagement is related broadly and deeply to the factors that impact all aspects of organizational vitality. No other psychological variable, including employee motivation, has demonstrated such an extensive and consistent impact on an organization's bottom line.

Factors That Affect Employee Engagement and Disengagement

In an effort to better understand the drivers of engagement, I went to the experts—people in the workforce. After explaining the concept of engagement, study participants were asked, "What causes you to become engaged or disengaged in your work?" What follows are representative lists of responses.

FACTORS THAT CAUSE EMPLOYEE ENGAGEMENT
- When I respect my employer or supervisor, when I respect the goals of the organization or the project, and when other people at work treat me with respect
- Trust; feeling that my supervisor has my back
- Feeling connected to the end result
- Knowing that what I do matters and can make a difference to others and to the business

- Feeling proud of my work
- Feeling a sense of empowerment and trust from my supervisor
- A supervisor who believes in me and wants me to excel
- A team that enjoys working with me and respects me
- Freedom to do my job and awareness that my contribution makes a difference
- Honesty and trust in management
- When my manager recognizes me and gives me credit for my work
- Respect for my opinion and trust in my abilities
- When I understand how and why the work matters
- When I have the tools to do my job properly
- When I feel I have a say in setting my goals and receive regular feedback from my supervisor about my performance
- Having a supervisor who does not feel it necessary to look over my shoulder
- The opportunity to learn new things at work and being given interesting things to do
- Having clear goals and objectives
- Having opportunities for promotion within the organization
- When I feel as though I am part of and needed by the organization and that my work is genuinely valued
- When I have freedom to determine how I achieve my goals
- Mutual and contagious respect among co-workers

If you want to increase employee engagement, you've got to understand what causes employees to increase their sense of commitment to the organization. In creating a model of employee engagement, it is equally important to understand the disengaged employee. It would be a mistake to assume that disengaged employees are simply the opposite of engaged employees. How do disengaged employees act, think, and feel? Without looking at both sides of the spectrum, it would be impossible to identify the psychological factors that distinguish engaged from disengaged employees.

Apathy is the hallmark of the disengaged employee whose mantra is "I don't care." Disengaged employees check their brains and hearts at the door. They take no pride in their work. Their primary concern is to figure out how little they can do and still collect a paycheck. *No organization ever achieved great things with people just going through the motions.* More than just apathetic, these individuals engage in activities that actively detract from the vitality of your organization. For example, they may knowingly withhold or give inaccurate information to customers and team members. They feel little, if any, sense of connection to their supervisor or organization. In fact, they likely speak poorly about team members, their supervisor, organizational leaders, and the organization as a whole. They are toxic to your culture—the proverbial "rotten apples."

As you can imagine, such employees are a financial drain on your organization. In fact, the Gallup Organization has suggested that disengaged employees around the globe cost companies hundreds of billions of dollars a year. According to a study published by Gallup in 2009, Germany is plagued by disengaged employees who are costing their country between 81 billion and 109 billion euros per year in lost productivity. The most disengaged employees are nearly impossible to rescue. Furthermore, doing so would require tremendous resources better spent on those with greater promise. Termination of extremely disengaged employees will have an immediate and positive impact on team vitality and productivity as others see that the offending team member was finally held accountable and let go.

Given the costs associated with employee disengagement, being able to prevent or curb it would be extremely valuable to any organization. Obviously, we need to begin with a clear understanding of the factors that lead to disengagement. Like the findings on causes for employee engagement, my research revealed many reasons why employees disengage, most having to do with the employee's direct supervisor. As you read the following list, notice how many of these issues could be easily prevented or resolved with basic supervisory coaching and training. Also, consider how much just one supervisor who creates a team of disengaged employees actually costs your organization.

FACTORS THAT CAUSE EMPLOYEE DISENGAGEMENT

- When my manager takes credit for my work
- Unrealistic expectations
- Lack of coaching, feedback, and support
- Incompetent leaders whom people don't respect
- Constantly being underappreciated and devalued
- Lack of basic pleasantries such as "hello" or "thank you"
- Lack of support from my manager
- Having to do work that doesn't appear to add value
- Seeing managers who are not actively engaged
- When a supervisor asks for an employee's opinion and then makes him or her feel stupid
- When a supervisor holds a meeting to get employee feedback and suggestions and doesn't follow up
- When your boss never asks for your input
- Lack of appreciation or compliments for a job well done
- Criticism that isn't constructive
- When you have no idea what direction the organization is headed
- Not being respected

- When you go above and beyond but your efforts are never recognized
- When you have to keep climbing over or around barriers to get what you need to do your job
- Overburdensome processes

What do you notice after reading this list? Were there any responses that were or were not on the list that surprised you? Were you surprised that money did not appear on the list? In all my research, less than 2 percent of respondents mentioned financial compensation as a cause of disengagement, and no one has ever mentioned it as a cause of engagement. What I notice most about these underlying reasons for disengagement is how relatively mundane and minor they are—not in the sense that they are unimportant, but rather how simply and easily most could be resolved with appropriate supervisory training. If Gallup is right and disengagement costs hundreds of billions of dollars in lost productivity, and these are the factors that cause disengagement, it seems like a no-brainer to allocate resources to address them. Why wouldn't you invest in a solution that paid back many times over?

If you're still not convinced that employee engagement presents a significant opportunity for you to grow the bottom line of your business, perhaps the research discussed next will lead you to that conclusion.

Employee Engagement Research

Given the financial implications of employee engagement, it's not surprising that a vast amount of research has been conducted on the subject over the past decade by many of the world's largest and most prestigious consulting firms, none more so than the Gallup

Organization. While it is not the intention of this book to provide a comprehensive review of all the research—Gallup's research alone would require its own book—I will share a sampling of the most compelling findings. This research clearly demonstrates the competitive advantage of organizations with high levels of employee engagement. (For a detailed review of the literature, see David MacLeod and Nita Clarke's 2009 report commissioned by the Department of Government, United Kingdom.)

Engagement Distribution

Gallup reports that 17 percent of American workers are "actively engaged," 29 percent "engaged," and 54 percent "not engaged." Using their own assessment instrument, U.S. Merit Systems Protection Board surveyed nearly thirty-seven thousand employees across twenty-four federal agencies and found that 35 percent of employees were "engaged," 47 percent "somewhat engaged," and 18 percent "not engaged." Using a four-level system, Towers Watson reports that 21 percent of employees are "engaged," 41 percent "enrolled," 30 percent "disenchanted," and 8 percent "disengaged." Using their proprietary model, Blessing White classified 29 percent of employees as "engaged," 27 percent "almost engaged," 19 percent "disengaged," 12 percent "Hamsters & Honeymooners," and 13 percent "Crash & Burners."

Retention and Turnover

Gallup's 2006 meta-analysis of 23,910 business units conducted by Dr. Jim Harter revealed that business units with scores in the bottom versus top quartile averaged 31 percent to 51 percent greater employee turnover. Consistent with Gallup's research, the Corporate Leadership Council's study of more than fifty thousand employees in twenty-nine companies showed that actively disengaged employees were nine times more likely to leave the organization than actively engaged employees. Towers

Watson found that 28 percent of disengaged employees are actively seeking new jobs compared to only 4 percent of engaged employees.

Productivity

Based on the Program Assessment Rating Tool (PART), which measures effectiveness of federal agencies to achieve their goal, agencies with the most-engaged employees scored an average of 65 (out of 100) while those agencies with the least-engaged employees received a score of 37 on the PART. Thus, agencies with the most-engaged employees were twice as successful in meeting their goals. Towers Watson's 2008–2009 WorkUSA Report found that highly engaged workers are 26 percent more productive than disengaged employees.

Profitability

Towers Watson studied fifty global companies over a one-year period. Companies with high employee engagement scores showed a 28 percent growth in earnings per share and 19 percent increase in operating income. In contrast, companies with the lowest levels of employee engagement scores saw an 11 percent drop in earnings per share and 32 percent drop in operating income. Gallup's research revealed that companies with engagement scores in the top quartile reported earnings per share 2.6 times higher than organizations with below-average scores. Towers Watson reported that companies with highly engaged employees earned 13 percent greater total returns for shareholders over a five-year period than companies with less engaged employees.

Absenteeism

Towers Watson's 2008–2009 WorkUSA Report found that highly engaged employees take 20 percent fewer sick days than their disengaged counterparts. Similarly, a 2008 report by the federal government found that among federal workers in the United States, disengaged employees take 25 percent more sick days than engaged employees.

Accidents

Federal agencies with the lowest average engagement scores compared to those with the highest experienced almost three times the average Occupational Safety and Health Administration (OSHA) lost-time case rate (.73 versus 2.15 per 100 employees). In a Towers Watson study at beverage giant Molson Coors, compared to engaged employees, disengaged employees were five times more likely to have a safety incident and seven times more likely to be involved in a lost-time safety incident. Moreover, the average cost of a safety incident was six times greater for the disengaged than engaged employees ($392 versus $63).

Equal Employment Opportunity (EEO) Complaints

Federal agencies with low employee engagement had more than double the EEO complaints of agencies with high levels of employee engagement (.47 percent versus 1.04 percent).

The Bottom Line

The research evidence in support of employee engagement as a critical determinant of organizational vitality is overwhelming and unanimous. Companies that foster high levels of employee engagement enjoy a measurable competitive advantage relative to those companies with policies, practices, and cultures that dissuade engagement. *The bottom line is that employee engagement contributes to the bottom line.* At the same time, I would be remiss in not drawing attention to a critical methodological problem common to nearly all studies, namely, the lack of a valid assessment instrument by which to measure employee engagement. If the assessment is invalid, then conclusions drawn from the research must be considered suspect.

Just Because You Call It Engagement Doesn't Make It Engagement

While writing this book, I contacted several of the largest consulting firms that claim expertise in the area of employee engagement. During an interview with one CEO, I shared my concerns regarding current research methods and asked his thoughts on defining engagement. He responded, "It is whatever you define it be." His answer represents both the exact state of affairs and the central problem. Dozens of different researchers and consultants are defining and measuring supposedly the same construct using completely different methods. In fact, MacLeod and Clarke's study identified more than fifty distinct definitions. No field of study can advance under these Tower of Babel conditions.

I am certainly not the first to identify this significant and widespread methodological problem. In an article published in 2008 in the journal *Industrial and Organizational Psychology*, Drs. William Macey and Benjamin Schneider wrote: "Most of the engagement measures we have seen failed to get the conceptualization correct. . . . Especially in the world of practice, we have seen measures of what we have called conditions for engagement labeled as measures of engagement (Buckingham & Coffman, 1999), and many measures used for years as indicators of employee opinions relabeled as indicants of employee engagement." *Just because you call it employee engagement doesn't make it employee engagement.*

The Root of the Problem

As the concept of employee engagement has grown in popularity, consultants have scrambled onto the engagement bandwagon to lay claim as experts in the field. In the words of John Gibbons of the Conference Board:

> *The difficulty in agreeing on what employee engagement actually is also stems from the efforts of competing consulting firms to create opinion surveys that represent their own unique approach to the concept. These consultants understandably have worked hard to create brandable approaches in order to distinguish themselves from their competitors. But, by doing so, they have in fact created a confusing number of de facto definitions of employee engagement. What's more, they have also created an equally diverse array of ways to measure it.*

Benjamin Schneider and his colleagues wrote: "The plurality of these engagement definitions make [*sic*] it obvious that the measurement of engagement is neither uniform nor clear. In fact, many HR consultants and practitioners have re-packaged existing employee surveys and called them engagement surveys." As a field of study and practice, this matter is not simply confusing . . . it is grave.

Lack of Accountability

You might wonder, given the magnitude of this problem and its implications, why consulting firms have not been held accountable for using valid measures of employee engagement. The reason is that most corporate vice presidents and human resources managers who engage consulting firms do not have a sufficient background in research methods and statistics to properly vet such instruments and naïvely assume that they are valid. Thus, resources are spent on invalid assessments, and frequently even greater resources are spent on follow-up interventions to increase the scores of an erroneous assessment. Unfortunately, there is no oversight committee or regulatory body that watches over consulting firms and requires them to demonstrate the validity of their instruments or services—buyer beware!

Defining Employee Engagement

It is difficult to overemphasize the critical importance of how one defines and measures a psychological construct. All research findings, conclusions, and subsequent interventions are based on the premise that you have accurately measured what you intended to measure. Psychological constructs, such as employee satisfaction, motivation, and engagement, are challenging to measure because they are composed of subjective feelings, thoughts, and beliefs that cannot be measured directly. There is no absolute scale or agreed-on instrument or test. The task is further complicated by the conceptual overlap among similar constructs. For example, employees who are engaged may also appear motivated and vice versa. Distinguishing similar constructs is critically important to advance our understanding of each as an individual factor, how they relate to one another, and how each can be affected.

Conceptual Definition of "Employee Engagement"

The first step in assessing a psychological construct is to create a conceptual definition that serves as the foundation on which the measurement instrument will be built. A conceptual definition describes in general terms the phenomenon under investigation using well-known and accepted descriptors. For example, we might define self-esteem as the extent to which a person holds positive feelings toward himself or herself. Think about the conceptual definition as the one that you might find in the dictionary. As mentioned earlier, more than fifty definitions have been identified for employee engagement. Fortunately, the Conference Board convened a committee of experts to address this very issue and created the following composite definition: "Employee engagement is a heightened emotional and intellectual connection that an employee has for his/her job, organization, manager, or coworkers that, in turn, influences him/her to apply additional discretionary effort to his/her work." Critically, this definition distinguishes among the four different areas—job, organization, manager, and co-workers—in which an employee may feel engaged, whereas many other definitions of engagement ignore this distinction. For those in sales or service organizations, I recommend including "client" as a fifth category to which employees may feel connected.

While the conceptual definition helps us to understand and speak about a phenomenon, it is the operational definition that helps us to measure the construct.

Operational Definition of "Employee Engagement"

There is no more basic or important methodological issue in all of science than how we measure the variables, terms, objects, and constructs that we study. W. Edwards Deming, considered the father of Total Quality Management and the driving force behind the success of Japanese manufacturing, wrote: "An operational definition is a procedure agreed upon for translation of concept into measurement." The operational definition allows for a common understanding and agreement of what is being measured and how it is being measured. Without such a process, the world would be in chaos. Just imagine if we could not agree on how to measure an acre of land, the length of a day, an ounce of gold, or the relative value of currencies around the world. All science, commerce, and trade would literally stop without the objective standards created by operational definitions.

In psychology, operational definitions are more challenging than they are in other fields because many of the phenomenons we investigate are not directly measurable. Our goal is to translate, or operationalize, the conceptual definition into specific items that we hope accurately and reliably assess the construct of interest. For example, if we wanted to operationalize "employee satisfaction," we might ask questions such as, "Do you enjoy coming to work?" "Are you happy in your current role?" and "Are you satisfied with your compensation?" Each of these questions is then used in creating the assessment instrument.

When generating items that define a construct, it becomes critical to remain tied as closely as possible to the conceptual definition to avoid overlapping with similar constructs. The goal is to create items that measure the entire construct and only that construct. It is at exactly this critical point, the operationalizing of engagement, that the wheels fall off most current research. Most often, researchers confuse and overlap items that more appropriately belong on a motivation or satisfaction survey rather than an engagement survey. Similarly, instead of measuring engagement itself, researchers often assess the factors that cause engagement to occur. My intent in the following section is to provide clarity to this issue and enable you to evaluate, at least in part, whether an employee engagement instrument meets criteria for construct validity.

Cause Versus Symptom

The primary challenge is to distinguish between what something *is* from its underlying *cause* or *conditions*. In the physical realm, this is an easy concept to grasp. You visit your doctor for your annual physical and she conducts a series of tests. Unfortunately, the tests reveal that you have elevated blood glucose levels and you will have to take medicine for diabetes. When you ask the doctor how this happened, she explains that there are many contributing factors including diet, weight, genetics, and exercise. In this example, these factors are not only relevant in understanding the underlying cause of the illness, but they may also prove helpful in managing it. To add to the confusion, people without any of these risk factors get diabetes. Thus, while understanding the causes are important, they are irrelevant to diagnosing whether one has diabetes. That's what the blood glucose test is for.

Now let's take a psychological example. Imagine creating a questionnaire to assess depression. Begin by asking yourself what does it feel or look like when someone is depressed. Based on your thoughts and experiences you might generate items such as: "Have you been feeling sad lately?" "Have you been feeling as though nothing matters?" and "Have you been sleeping more or less than usual?" These questions reflect symptoms indicative of depression. In developing your assessment instrument you would not ask, "Did you recently get into a fight with your significant other?" or "Did you recently receive bad news from your doctor?" While these issues, as well as thousands of others, might trigger a depressive episode and be relevant to understanding and treating the patient, they are totally irrelevant in determining whether someone meets the criteria for depression.

The valid assessment of a psychological construct is based on identifying the symptoms, not the causes.

Now, imagine creating a survey for employee engagement. Ask yourself, "What are the *symptoms* of engagement?" (I realize that "symptoms" may sound odd in this context, but please stay with me.) To answer this, think about a time when you were highly engaged in your work and recall your associated thoughts, feelings, and behaviors. Just like the study participants, think about engaged employees you've known and what they looked like. What was it in their actions or words that made you consider them engaged? Just as important, consider what disengagement looks and feels like. The answers to these questions will help you to identify appropriate items for an engagement survey.

Personally, when I'm engaged in my work, the day passes by very quickly. When I'm disengaged, I'm typically quite bored and watch the clock. When I'm engaged, I tend to go the extra mile and do more than the job requires; when I'm disengaged I do only what is necessary to get the job done. When I feel highly engaged with a project, I find myself thinking about it all the time—inside and outside of work; when I'm not engaged, I think about the project only when I'm on the clock. For me, these are some of the "symptoms" that let me know when I am engaged or disengaged. I encourage you to take a moment to write down your own thoughts.

In creating items for your instrument, be careful to include only items that directly measure engagement and not similar constructs or the underlying causes of engagement. As we discussed earlier, many factors impact a person's level of engagement, such as having a supportive supervisor, receiving appropriate recognition, doing meaningful work, and being shown respect, but these are not symptoms of employee engagement and thus shouldn't be included in the assessment.

> While identifying the underlying causes of employee engagement
> and disengagement are important, they are not appropriate to
> include in an instrument that claims to measure engagement.

To summarize, symptoms provide evidence of the phenomenon, while causes give you possible explanations of why the phenomenon occurred in the first place. The more that an employee engagement measure contains items relevant to related constructs such as employee satisfaction and motivation, and the more items there are that assess *causes* instead of *symptoms* of engagement, the less valid the measure. The less valid the measure, the less credible any findings or results that come from research using the instrument.

Although all psychological instruments should be evaluated across several forms of validity (e.g., construct, statistical, internal, external) and reliability (e.g., test-retest, parallel forms, internal consistency), this "symptom versus cause" distinction should enable you to readily distinguish the wheat from the chaff. I have spent several years creating an instrument that I believe identifies the symptoms of engagement. Interested readers are invited to contact me directly (drpaul@therespectmodel .com) to receive a free copy of my employee engagement survey and scoring instructions.

Despite the widespread conceptual confusion and measurement problem, the construct of employee engagement remains valid. However, the field is in desperate need of individuals and organizations less concerned with marketing and selling engagement tools or programs and more concerned with developing measures and interventions based on sound empirical research.

My hope is that this chapter has helped to raise your awareness of these critical issues and made you a more educated consumer of psychological surveys and instruments in general. In the next chapter we synthesize the findings of our research on the factors that impact employee engagement and introduce the RESPECT Model.

CHAPTER 4 The RESPECT Model: Building a Culture of Employee Engagement

"Your job gives you authority. Your behavior gives you respect."

—Irwin Federman, general partner at
U.S. Venture Partners

Respect is the cornerstone of both our personal and our professional relationships and the *sine qua non* of employee engagement. Without respect, relationships don't work.

As our level of respect grows for an individual, so does our level of engagement. And when we lose respect, we disengage. It is difficult, if not impossible, to feel a sense of commitment to a person, team, or organization that one disrespects. There are many reasons why we gain and lose respect for people. For example, we may gain respect for a team member when we find out that she does substantial volunteer work, has overcome some challenging life circumstance or disability, just adopted a child with special needs, or is a veteran of the armed forces. Anytime we gain respect for others, we find ourselves being drawn to them. We want to be associated with people we respect. Alternatively, we lose respect for people when we learn that they have acted in an unscrupulous manner, for example, had an affair, spread gossip, or taken credit for another's work.

The concept of respect transcends time and culture. Throughout history, civilizations have created rituals to show respect to their gods, animals, and nature. In fact, cave drawings reflect early man's respect for the animals that sustained them. American Indians are renowned for their respect of Mother Earth and the animals they hunt. People kill and are willing to be killed over the issue of respect. Being disrespected even has its own slang term that has made its way into our vernacular—"dissed." If you don't think respect matters, just talk to a friend with a disrespectful teenager at home. Or, more relevantly, consider your reaction to being treated disrespectfully at work. Given the importance of this concept, how exactly do we get respect?

How Do We Get Respect?

There are two fundamental and very different approaches to getting respect. The first approach involves fear and intimidation—"You'll respect me because if you don't I'll hurt you or allow someone else to hurt you." The second approach, which I will call authentic respect, has little to do with controlling or manipulating others and is epitomized by "I'll respect you because that is who I am." However, with such respect does come great power and the ability to influence others. Mahatma Gandhi, Mother Theresa, Martin Luther King, Abraham Lincoln, and Jesus Christ fall into this category. These leaders inspire loyal followers who willingly exert extraordinary levels of effort to help fulfill their leader's vision. Unlike their tyrant counterparts, they demonstrate great respect for their followers. In organizations, these leaders engage the hearts and minds of all those around them. Who are the leaders you most respect? Are you that kind of leader?

A Profile of Respect

At the top of my personal list of most respected leaders is Dr. Edward Palmer, chair of the psychology department at Davidson College. I can say without hesitation that Ed would appear near the top of the list of anyone who knew him well. Although he is an accomplished and respected academic scholar and teacher, these are not the primary reasons for the respect he garners. Not to be unkind, but he's also not known for his physical prowess, scintillating personality, or stylish dress. In fact, if you passed Ed on the street or saw him at a party, it is unlikely that you would pay him much attention. Although his footprint is small, his impact on those around him has been profound.

Ed is a human being of unparalleled generosity, kindness, humility, and compassion. Whether it is a student struggling with his studies, a concerned parent, a colleague seeking his wise counsel, or a member of the janitorial staff looking to chat, Ed's door is always open. He listens with greater sincerity and more fully than anyone I've ever known. When you leave Ed's office, you feel completely understood and cared about. The full extent of his kindness and generosity is unknown because much of his charity is done when no one is watching. He's sneaky like that. I do know that if you need a car, he'll lend you his and may even give it to you; if you need a place to stay, he's got a spare room in his home for as long as you need; if he finds out that your family could use food, there will be groceries at your door; and, when you need it most of all, Ed takes you for a double scoop of ice cream at Carolina Cones.

That's the thing about Ed—you don't have to ask. When he finds out that you need help, he doesn't ask what he can do, he just does it. In 2007, Davidson College received the American Psychological Association's inaugural Departmental Award for the Culture of Service in the Psychological Sciences. Not surprisingly, the department has named this award the Edward L. Palmer Psychology Award, to honor and commemorate "the countless ways in which his life and work have graced others, professionally and personally."

I am not sharing this story simply because Ed is a wonderful human being; I am sharing it because he is a highly effective leader who engages the hearts and minds of everyone around him. If you have ever had the pleasure of being led by a person of Ed Palmer's character, you would then know that whatever he asked of you, you would do. And, you would do so not because it had anything to do with your job description but because you respect, believe, and trust in him and the thought of letting him down would be unthinkable. The essence of being a powerful and effective leader is having loyal followers who willingly do what is asked of them. Such real and enduring power cannot be demanded or coerced. It comes from a lifetime of quietly caring about, respecting, and serving others.

My education, research, and experience have led me to conclude that powerful leaders who create highly engaged employees do so by fostering a culture of respect in their organizations. It is through this lens that I created, and now share with you, the RESPECT Model.

The RESPECT Model

The RESPECT Model is an actionable philosophy based on the simple principle that when people are treated with respect they engage and work harder to achieve the goals of the organization. Over the past few years, a handful of researchers from around the world have empirically supported this premise, most notably Ed Sleebos, Naomi Ellemers, and Dick de Gilder from the Netherlands. These researchers have demonstrated in both laboratory and field studies that when people feel respected, they exhibit greater discretionary effort in order to benefit the group and organization. In addition, their research uncovered that when disrespected individuals exhibit discretionary effort, they do so to achieve personal gain—not to advance the goals of their group. These findings validate the basic premise of the RESPECT Model and highlight the distinction between engaged employees who work for the betterment of the organization and motivated employees who work for themselves.

What is an actionable philosophy? An actionable philosophy is a set of values or beliefs intended to guide one's daily actions and behaviors, for example, the Golden Rule, which teaches people to treat one another as they would want to be treated.

Circle of RESPECT

Based on engagement research, the Circle of RESPECT distinguishes five areas in which employees experience feelings of respect and disrespect.

- **Organization**—its mission, vision, values, goals, policies, and actions. Employees are proud to say, "I work for *this* organization."
- **Leadership**—especially as it concerns their direct supervisor, believing that he or she is competent and ethical, makes good decisions, and treats people fairly.
- **Team members**—believing that they are competent, cooperative, honest, supportive, and willing to pull their own weight.
- **Work**—finding it challenging, rewarding, interesting, and as having value to both internal and external customers.
- **Individual**—feeling respected by the organization, supervisor, and fellow team members.

Next to each area of the Circle of RESPECT (Figure 4.1) you will find a line. On that line, write down the time in your life when you experienced the greatest level of respect in each area. For example, I had tremendous respect for my colleagues at Davidson College, so on the line for Team Members I would write down: "Davidson, 1997–2000."

If it turns out that you have the same answer on all five lines, congratulations—not many people do, and I hope you are in that position right now. For those so fortunate, I bet you are excited to go to work, energized while there, and feel like what you do makes a difference. I'll bet you work hard but it doesn't much seem like work. I'll bet you're proud to tell people where you work and what you do. I'll also bet that you would describe

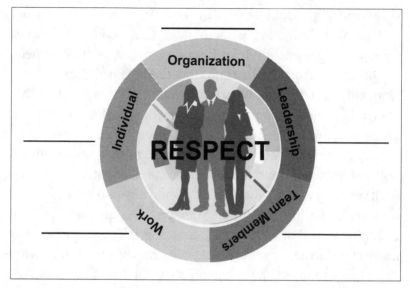

Figure 4.1 Circle of RESPECT

yourself as engaged and have no interest in leaving your organization. For everyone else, how many times did your current job top your list? If the answer is zero, I'm going to guess that you have felt more engaged at other points in your career and that you may even be considering a job move. While completing the Circle of RESPECT, what factors and experiences played into your answers? What led you to experience respect in each of these areas? We will examine the most prominent factors that typically increase or decrease respect in the following sections.

Respect for the Organization

Perceived organizational respect has an enormous impact on human capital and employee engagement. Research conducted by Zoe Barsness and her colleagues from the University of Washington shows that during the interview process people consider the pride and respect they anticipate feeling if they were to join a particular group. Research by Tom Tyler and Steve Blader of New York University demonstrates that people experience "group engagement" and work harder in groups they respect. In addition, a study by Lakshmi Ramarajan, Sigal Barsade, and Orah Burack from the Wharton School of Business finds that respecting one's organization serves as a buffer to burnout. Thus, compared to less respected organizations, those perceived as being highly respected enjoy a significant competitive advantage in terms of recruitment, employee productivity, and tenure. Another competitive advantage to being a well-respected organization is the likelihood that your products and services will be highly valued and trusted by consumers. This is particularly important during uncertain economic times when customers are more likely to question a company's stability: Will the organization still be in operation in ten years? Will it stand by its work? Does it cut corners?

The Importance of a Good Reputation The Reputation Institute based in New York City has been ranking companies around the world for the past ten years. Their research suggests that strong corporate reputations are based on four concepts: admiration, trust, good feelings, and overall esteem. Among the factors that increase an organization's reputation are giving back to the community and transparency in business dealings. Although I was unaware of this research by the Reputation Institute when I founded ColorMe Company in 2003, I knew instinctively that such values would not only enhance the reputation of my organization but also increase the respect of those who joined my team. Thus, I built the company on the principle that giving is good and established a unique and transparent policy in which 10 percent of *gross* proceeds were donated to children's charities. Although I never anticipated it, ColorMe Company was featured in a 2007 *Wall Street Journal* article on companies that give back. *Giving back always pays forward.*

Some organizations by the nature of their business are more likely to be well respected by their employees and community. Nonprofit organizations are an obvious category, as well as those organizations whose products and services make a significant contribution to the world. Johnson & Johnson has been one of my largest clients and a consumer of the RESPECT Model for several years. They also ranked first among American companies in the Reputation Institute's 2009 study. Organizational respect leads directly to discretionary effort; the more employees respect their organization, the harder they will work.

Here's the thing: you don't have to be a Johnson & Johnson to inspire your employees. It doesn't matter what your service or product, or how large your organization, you can still act in ways that increase your employees' respect. Companies that are socially responsible and positively impact their communities engender such feelings. Increasing your employees' respect for your organization does not require expensive or elaborate undertakings. For example, my local dry cleaner collects used winter coats, and then cleans and donates them to those in need. Some companies organize teams to work with Habitat for Humanity, hold blood donor drives, or allow employees to take volunteer days. A rock quarry with whom I worked donated materials and labor to build a new park for neighborhood children. Employees take pride in knowing that they work for a company that cares about people and their community. Every organization has the potential to help others and, in the process, earn the respect of its employees.

Tips for a Great Community Service Project While donating money to good causes is admirable, doing so will have far less impact on increasing employee pride than involving your employees in a community service project. In addition, such events often become powerful team-building experiences during which people form bonds and break boundaries in ways that simply cannot occur in an office environment. Although the work is to help others, the organization benefits greatly in the process. Here are a few tips to consider while planning community service projects:

1. Involve your employees right from the start by having them submit suggestions. Elect an employee committee to review and select the project. Consider making a small financial or product/service donation to charities that were not selected.
2. Focus on projects that can be completed in one day. People feel best and take the greatest pride in seeing projects from beginning to end. If beginning and finishing the entire project in one day is not possible, such as with building a house, try being responsible for one identifiable part, such as putting up the frame.
3. The more concrete and longer lasting the outcome of the effort, the more inspiring. For example, picking up trash along a highway is great, but it doesn't have nearly the same long-term impact as helping to construct a playground or planting trees. People want to point to something and say, "I helped do that."
4. Make sure that the project is well coordinated and organized. Find the best project managers in the company and enroll them in planning and organizing the event. There's nothing worse than people showing up to do a community service project and then just standing around drinking coffee.

5. Figure out how to create cross-departmental teams to work together that day. Use this as an opportunity for people who don't normally spend time together to get to know one another. This will create long-term, tangible benefits for your organization in terms of improved communication and partnering.

6. Record the event. Ask someone to videotape and take pictures; get at least one shot of everyone involved in the event. You will be able to use these images for multiple purposes such as the company newsletter, marketing materials, and year-end celebrations.

7. Get media attention. This is not about "Hey, look at us! We're such a great company." It is about increasing the pride of your employees. Imagine their sense of pride when their friends see the story run in the local paper and think, "Wow, that is so cool of your company; I wish my company would do something like that."

8. As always, the members of your organization's leadership team should serve as role models and demonstrate their support for the project by being the first to show up and the last to leave. Having the CEO show up just to shake hands and have pictures taken is insulting and demeaning to the project and efforts of your employees.

Be a Winner We all want to be on a winning team. Employees want to take pride in knowing that their company is doing something better than its competitors. The actual arena of competition, whether technology, innovation, efficiency, customer service, market share, profitability, or quality, is less important than that they are "the best" at something. Find those areas in which your organization excels relative to others and advertise it to your employees to boost their sense of pride and respect. Similarly, within an organization, employees want to know that there is something special about their team, department, or business unit. Again, the more people respect and take pride in their group, the harder they will work to help the group achieve success. Without creating conflicts among departments, is there a particular area your employees can be recognized for and feel good about? Thus, look for "low-hanging fruit" opportunities that could boost the self-esteem of your team members. In general, always be on the lookout for ways to make people feel good about and take pride in their organization.

Respect for the Supervisor

The more employees respect their supervisor, the more engaged they will be in their work. Several factors affect employees' perceptions, beginning with the supervisor's own work ethic. Employees respect and work hard for competent and hardworking supervisors. Supervisors who are promoted from within an organization are often highly respected and credible because they have done the jobs of their employees and can offer tangible assistance. This is particularly important when it comes to giving employees corrective feedback and conducting performance evaluations.

Supervisors also gain respect when they are strong enough to hold the line and do the right thing in the face of opposition. Employees want a supervisor who is a leader willing to stand up to upper management and who uses his or her influence for the betterment of the team and organization. Particularly in difficult times, supervisors gain respect for holding teams together and for focusing their teams on working together to accomplish their goals.

To be respected, supervisors must be viewed as fair, trustworthy, honest, committed, and compassionate. They must possess sufficient interpersonal and communication skills to develop rapport and build positive relations with employees. Critically, supervisors must be viewed as advocates for their employees as well as the organization. Whenever supervisors denigrate an employee or the organization, they lose respect. I encourage you to examine your own behaviors—as well as those of supervisors whom you have respected—and look for opportunities to improve your relations and reputation with your employees.

Respect for Team Members

Highly productive teams will always have one thing in common: team members who respect one another. Productivity results from team members working cohesively and synergistically with one another. When employees respect their team members, they often increase their own efforts as they seek to be respected by their co-workers. Employees lose respect for team members whom they perceive as unskilled, uncooperative, or underperforming. Loss of respect is accompanied by frustration and disengagement. Often, supervisors contribute to this situation by failing to hold underperforming team members accountable.

Team members lose respect for one another and the team becomes dysfunctional and less productive when employees start speaking *about* one another instead of *to* one another. When team members respect one another, they resolve conflicts by speaking directly to each other about their concerns. Organizations that have established a policy that encourages employees not to speak disparagingly of co-workers are dramatically more productive.

Increasing respect among team members (or any group of people) is quite simple. Psychologically, the more that people have in common, the more they like one another. When team members have the opportunity to learn more about one another, they often uncover areas of commonality such as where they grew up, what their parents did, favorite hobbies, or having children of the same age. It takes very little for people to feel more connected to one another; naturally, the more unusual the common denominator, the stronger the sense of connectedness. There is another important reason that learning more about people is important. A better understanding of someone's background often leads to more tolerance, compassion, and understanding. In fact, just a single piece of information might completely change the lens through which you look at someone and interpret his or her actions.

Over the years I have created an exercise called "Your Story" that I use to begin all RESPECT Team Building sessions. The exercise is a series of questions about one's life. Although the issues are not overly personal, participants may skip any they prefer not to address. Sample questions include, "Where were you born and raised?" "What is the most adventurous or dangerous thing you've done?" and "What is the best career advice you ever received?" (I have included the full list of questions and directions for implementing the exercise in the Appendix.) Each time I facilitate this exercise, I am reminded that people who have worked with one another for long periods of time actually know little about each other. Moreover, I am amazed by the impact of this sharing on people's relationships. Team members always leave this session with a greater understanding and appreciation for one another. Moreover, relationships typically grow beyond this session as team members find reasons to get together outside of work based on their newly discovered common interests or activities. Your Story is a free, easy-to-facilitate exercise that will have a significant impact on your team members' respect for one another and engagement to their group.

Respect for the Work

Has a supervisor ever asked you to do a task that you know is absolutely meaningless and far beneath your skill level? If so, then you know how de-motivating this can feel. For people to respect their work they must find it challenging, meaningful, and rewarding. The more that a task requires an individual to utilize his or her full complement of skills, the more challenging and engaging that person finds the work. Successful completion of challenging work engenders feelings of pride and accomplishment. This is why hiring someone who is overqualified is a bad idea; almost invariably they resent doing work beneath their qualifications, are bored, and will quit as soon as they have a better opportunity. It is also the reason that supervisors and employers must continually look for ways to keep their employees challenged. Cross-training is an excellent way to keep team members challenged and engaged, increase camaraderie and collaboration, and create a more flexible and efficient team.

The extent to which an employee finds a task meaningful can be increased in a number of ways. First, their assignment must be aligned with organizational goals. If corporate marching orders have everyone working on X and you are asked to work on Y, then you're going to wonder how what you're doing fits into the bigger picture. Employees want to know that what they are doing matters and that it is relevant to the organization's mission. Second, tasks become meaningful and employee pride increases when supervisors explicitly assign tasks to individual employees because they trust that they are best suited for the particular work. Hearing your boss say, "Barbara, I'm asking you to do this because I think you're the best person for the job" trumps, "Yeah, everyone else was busy." People also tend to have greater respect for a task when they teach it to others. Thus, asking team members to cross-train one another can increase task value and also the respect felt by the employees doing the training. Finally, the task becomes significant when successful completion leads to additional opportunities.

The less intrinsic motivation the task holds—the less challenging it is for the employee, the less it is identified as making a difference, or the less connected to an overall outcome—the more important it is that the supervisor take the time to explain why the task is indeed important. When a supervisor communicates the importance of a task, the psychological value of that task increases. To be clear, I am not suggesting that you pull a Tom Sawyer and turn your organization's equivalent of whitewashing a fence into some glamorous opportunity. If it is simply one of those jobs that needs to be done, don't make up an elaborate story. Just be honest. Unfortunately, most supervisors don't bother helping employees to understand the importance of their work and its connection to the big picture. To remain fully engaged, employees must leave work every day feeling that they have contributed in a meaningful way to the organization and its goals. Do your employees feel this way?

Feeling Respected as an Individual

The most important question that predicts an employee's engagement is, Do you feel respected by those in your organization? The more employees feel valued, appreciated, and respected, the greater their level of engagement and discretionary effort. People want to work for honest organizations that treat them with consideration, fairness, and respect. Such organizations are rewarded with loyal and engaged employees. Of course the opposite is true as well. Organizations that lay people off, freeze pay, cut health-care benefits, and reduce retirement benefits while simultaneously awarding C-level executives generous bonuses will be left with a highly disgruntled, disaffected, and disengaged workforce. Organizations cannot complain about high turnover rates and lack of employee loyalty when they make such blatantly disrespectful decisions. And it happens all the time.

There is an old saying: "Do right by people and they'll do right by you." I don't hear that expression much anymore, especially in a difficult economy that makes it easy for bad supervisors to tell employees, "You should feel lucky to have a job." I'm certain that hearing that from my supervisor would fire me up, but probably just not in the way he or she intended. There are still companies out there that have strong cultures imbued with the philosophy of doing right by their people. One of them is Mannington Mills, headquartered in Salem, New Jersey. The privately held, fourth-generation company was founded in 1915 and produces residential and commercial flooring. Their corporate culture and philosophy are well articulated by their vision, mission, and values statements, which I encourage you to read in full by visiting their website (mannington.com). Two of their core values are: "To care about one another, value and respect each other's rights, and foster an environment of fairness," and "To do the right thing always acting in the best interests of all, never misleading or distorting the truth." The difference I find between Mannington and a lot of other companies is that they actually live their values and use them in making business decisions, especially the tough ones. Their adherence to their corporate values may help explain why the average employee tenure is fifteen years and they have virtually no voluntary turnover.

Seven Drivers of RESPECT Model

In my research, I identified respect as the central driving force behind engagement. I also identified several specific factors that cause employees to feel respected. Using the word *respect* as an acronym, the RESPECT Model is defined by seven critical drivers that influence an employee's internal assessment of respect and subsequent level of engagement:

Recognition: Employees feel acknowledged and appreciated for their contributions. Supervisors regularly recognize deserving team members, and people are rewarded based on their work performance.

Empowerment: Supervisors provide employees with the tools, resources, and training to succeed. Employees experience high levels of autonomy and are encouraged to take risks. Supervisors take the initiative to communicate with employees and ensure that they are equipped to succeed, not fail.

Supportive feedback: Supervisors provide employees with timely, specific feedback in a supportive, sincere, and constructive manner. Feedback is delivered for the purpose of reinforcement and improvement—never to embarrass or punish.

Partnering: Employees are treated as business partners and actively collaborate in business-making decisions. They receive financial information, understand the big picture, and are given wide latitude in decision making. Supervisors serve as advocates for their employees' development and growth. Team members and departments actively communicate and share information with one another.

Expectations: Supervisors ensure that goals, objectives, and business priorities are clearly established and communicated. Employees know precisely the standards by which their performance is evaluated and are held accountable for meeting their performance expectations.

Consideration: Supervisors, managers, and team members demonstrate consideration, caring, and thoughtfulness toward one another. Supervisors actively seek to understand employees' opinions and concerns and are understanding and supportive when employees experience personal problems.

Trust: Supervisors demonstrate trust and confidence in employees' skills and abilities. Employees trust that their supervisor will do right by them. Leaders keep their promises and commitments and, in return, are trusted by employees.

Each of these drivers contributes uniquely to the employees' overall experience of being respected and influences their level of engagement. In the chapters that follow, we will explore each driver in detail, beginning with an overview of the concept, a brief self-assessment quiz, and a list of benefits realized from being proficient in that driver. And to help you apply the concept in your organization right away, each chapter contains specific, concrete strategies and tips. Remember, RESPECT is about a way of being and behaving and is intended to change the culture of your organization from the top down. Leaders who commit to learning and following the tenets and principles of this model will transform their organization's culture and realize unprecedented results in employee engagement and productivity.

CHAPTER 5 Recognition

> "There are two things people want more than
> sex and money . . . recognition and praise."
> —*Mary Kay Ash, founder of Mary Kay Cosmetics*

N o finding in all of psychology and human resources is more consistent than the positive impact of recognition on employee performance. Fundamentally, people simply want to be recognized and acknowledged for their efforts and contributions. Whether at work, among friends, or with our significant other, we want to know that what we do matters and is appreciated. Although there are many forms of acknowledgment, the most powerful is social reinforcement, that is, praise. In our research, people overwhelmingly identified a simple thank you as the most important and meaningful form of recognition.

Unfortunately, many managers don't feel as though they should have to thank employees for doing their jobs. Moreover, supervisors consistently overrate the extent to which they give recognition and underrate the extent to which it is valued by employees. Thus, providing recognition to employees presents an immediate opportunity to increase discretionary effort. In truth, supervisors who fail to take a few minutes a day to recognize employees are not doing their job responsibly or effectively. How do you rate when it comes to showing your employees respect through recognition? Take the following quiz and find out.

RECOGNITION SELF-ASSESSMENT QUIZ

Instructions: Read each statement below and decide how accurately it describes your behavior using the following scale:

a. **Never or rarely engage in this behavior (0 points)**
b. **Sometimes engage in this behavior (1 point)**
c. **Regularly engage in this behavior (2 points)**
d. **Always or almost always engage in this behavior (3 points)**

Place the point value of your answer choice on the blank line at the beginning of the statement.

_____ 1. **I acknowledge and thank at least one person a day for his or her work on a specific task.**

_____ 2. **In the past month, I have thanked every employee in my department for the work that he or she does either in person, over the phone, or with a handwritten note.**

_____ 3. **When I see an employee who is not in my department do a good job, I make sure to let his or her boss know.**

_____ 4. **When one of my employees does a great job, I request that my boss call to recognize that employee directly.**

_____ **5. I take time during each team meeting to publicly acknowledge individuals for their recent good work.**

_____ **Total Number of Points**

INTERPRETING YOUR SCORES

0-5: Supervisors who score in this range are actively diminishing the human capital of their organization. It is not just that employees do not feel respected; they feel disrespected. As a result, you and your organization are realizing only a fraction of the discretionary effort possible by your employees. Increasing your skills in the area of recognition should be an immediate priority.

6-10: Your mediocre recognition score will result in mediocre engagement and performance relative to the potential of your employees. Look for more regular opportunities to "catch employees doing good," especially those employees who may be average performers and frequently overlooked. It is among the average employees that you have the greatest opportunity to increase the productivity of your department and organization.

11-15: Scores in this range suggest that you are regularly acknowledging your employees' contributions and maximizing the human capital in your organization. Your employees feel respected and will repay you with high levels of discretionary effort. Work to shape specific behaviors in individual employees through selective and varied social reinforcement. Also, consider giving advice and guidance to other supervisors in your organization who could benefit from increasing their skills in this area.

Benefits of Recognizing Your Employees

The greatest specific benefit of recognition is its ability to replicate behavior, that is, make it more likely to occur again. Critically, reinforcement makes the behavior more likely to occur again unprompted. In other words, *today's reinforcement creates tomorrow's initiative*. Thank an employee for going out of his way to take care of a customer and he will do so again. Acknowledge a team member for taking the initiative to train a new colleague on the computer system and she will take such initiative again. There is simply nothing more important or valuable to a business than the employee who takes initiative instead of sitting around waiting to be told what to do. Whatever behavior you pay attention to you get more of; the principle of recognition is as powerful as it is simple.

I know of no other strategy in all of management that yields a higher return on investment. In my estimate, the ROI is 1:100. In other words, for every minute spent on reinforcing behavior, you can expect a hundred minutes of initiative in return. The following example portrays the real-world benefit of recognizing and reinforcing employees. Imagine being out of the office for a meeting and calling to check in with your team. If you're the kind of manager who has taken the time to recognize and acknowledge team members, you get: "Hey boss, we had a problem, but we took care of it." If you've failed to recognize your employees, you get: "Hey boss, we've got a problem." Which call do you have with your employees?

So What if I Don't Recognize?

Nearly everyone knows that reinforcing behavior through praise makes it more likely to occur again. Whether you're praising an employee, child, or pet, it works. What most people don't understand is that failing to reinforce behavior actually makes it less likely to happen in the future. For example, imagine asking an employee to stay late to help with a project. He does so and you don't bother saying thanks. The next time that you ask him to stay late, he will be less likely to do so because he feels unappreciated.

The same principle applies to correcting problem behaviors. Imagine that you have an employee who is chronically five minutes late to work. You decide to speak with her to discuss the impact that being late has on team members, to explain that it doesn't fit with the company's culture and values, and to clearly set the expectation that she will be on time. The next few days the employee is on time and you say nothing. In the absence of praise for being on time, the employee will be at much greater risk for slipping back into her old habit of being late. When do most supervisors say something? Yep, the next time she is late! Here's what you need to know: *you will never get the behavior you want by focusing on the behavior you don't want*. For example, you don't get team members to take initiative by focusing on their lack of initiative. Focusing on problematic behaviors is called nagging and, while annoying, it is ineffective. To fundamentally change behavior, you must use positive reinforcement and focus on the behavior that you do want, not the behavior that you don't want. Later in this chapter I'll describe in detail about how to do just that.

Employees come to us in a state of readiness to engage, and it is the behavior and decisions of managers and organizational leaders that can result in even the best employees becoming disengaged over time. Although the rate of disengagement can be rapid, as in my own experience that I shared earlier, the descent is typically more gradual and results from managers who fail to acknowledge their employees' contributions over time. Such employees feel taken for granted and disrespected. Have you ever worked for a boss who rarely, if ever, recognized your hard work? The following example about Peter exemplifies the cost of failing to acknowledge your employees.

Story from the Trenches

Peter was a bright, hardworking, and dedicated young human resources consultant; he had all the "right stuff." He consistently went above and beyond the expectations of both his boss and his clients. He cared about doing things right and never complained about putting in long hours or staying behind to finish work while the boss took clients to dinner. Peter's efforts were noticed by clients, which led to more work and money for his company. By all measures, Peter was doing well.

I met Peter after delivering a presentation on the RESPECT Model. He said, "I just wanted to thank you; I came here today with a question and you answered it." I told him that I was glad to have helped and asked if he would share the question. He said, "I've been with the same company for several years. I've done well and have been pretty happy, but over the last several months I've grown more and more disengaged. I haven't felt as energized as I once did and don't work as hard anymore. Honestly, I just don't care as much as I used to, and, before today, I couldn't figure out why. What I realized from your talk is that I just haven't felt respected. In all the years that I've worked for my boss, I don't remember him ever telling me that he really appreciated my efforts."

Peter contacted me shortly after we spoke. He had decided to call one of the many clients who had offered him a job over the years. When he submitted his resignation, his boss was in complete shock and said, "I don't understand. You've done so well here. You're such a great asset to this company." Peter's company lost a great employee because his manager failed to engage in the most basic tenet of the RESPECT Model, namely, to recognize and acknowledge employees for their contributions.

I Don't Praise Because . . .

Despite the overwhelming evidence demonstrating the importance of recognizing employees, supervisors and managers continue to have a plethora of excuses for not doing so. Here is a list of common excuses given by supervisors for not recognizing employees and my responses to them:

1. **"I don't have the time."** This is by far the most frustrating response because people that say this fundamentally don't understand the impact of praise. Effectively recognizing an employee typically takes a few seconds or perhaps a minute. How long does it take to write a note or an e-mail that says, "Tom, I just wanted to say really great job with that presentation this morning"? If you went all out and stopped by an employee's office space to thank her in person, how long would that take? If you're really concerned about saving thirty seconds, you can make your feedback a stop on your way back from lunch.

2. **"I shouldn't have to thank my employees for doing their jobs."** Try to change your mind-set so that you view employee recognition as part of your job. The most important job of any leader is to increase the value of the company's human resources. Recognizing employees increases their discretionary effort and, in turn, increases the human capital of the organization. Moreover, if you fail to recognize your employees, they lose respect and become less productive. If your own philosophical beliefs about work prevent you from acknowledging your employees, then you need to stop managing people.

3. **"It's not my personality."** It's not in my personality to wash dishes, exercise regularly, or maintain my car. I do those things because they make my life work. Praising employees works. Supervisors need not act like high school cheerleaders; they simply have to sincerely acknowledge employees' contributions. While one supervisor might high-five an employee and say, "Way to go!" another might simply shake hands and say, "Thank you." You don't need to change your core personality to effectively recognize employees.

4. **"I don't want to manipulate other people."** This one always makes me laugh. We are constantly manipulating other people because we are always "consequating" their behavior. In other words, how we respond or don't respond to others affects them. Imagine saying hello to your boss as you see her walking toward you and all the possible responses. She might rush by you and say nothing, say hello back, or stop and ask about your weekend. Of course, there are numerous possible scenarios and we haven't even considered the impact of *how* she might have spoken to you, including tone of voice or various nonverbal factors such as eye contact. So, when your boss walks by and gives a quick "Hey" while reading her Blackberry, is she trying to manipulate you with her response? Of course

not. Do these different responses impact you? Of course. You can call it manipulating others if you like, but the point is that we are constantly affecting others' thoughts, behaviors, and feelings based on what we do and say. Wouldn't it be better to understand the impact of your actions and use them strategically to make your employees feel more appreciated and respected?

5. **"I don't see my employees enough; we are at different locations."** You don't need to physically see your employees to praise them. Use the phone, send e-mail, or write a short note. Your efforts will mean more because the employee recognizes the challenges of connecting in person. Sales representatives who cover physical territories are particularly prone to feeling disconnected and unappreciated; they need extremely committed supervisors willing to be resourceful and do what it takes to connect with and recognize these employees.

6. **"I have too many employees."** Being able to regularly praise more than twenty-five direct reports is challenging. In such cases, you need to enroll and train foremen and team leaders to recognize and reinforce good behavior. Encourage all team members to bring to your attention an employee who goes above and beyond. Use highly efficient methods of praise, for example, morning or afternoon huddle meetings to praise individuals or teams publicly. My personal favorite is to use my travel time to call and thank employees.

Another suggestion is to focus your energy. For example, you could select one particular theme to reinforce over the course of a month, such as safety, and just be on the lookout for behaviors related to that theme. Obviously, having many employees is a challenge, but you can still be effective at recognizing good behavior. By the way, when you do praise employees, they will be especially appreciative because they realize how challenging it is to manage such a large staff; it means even more to receive praise from a boss managing forty people than four.

7. **"I don't get any recognition from *my* boss!"** As the old saying goes, two wrongs don't make a right. Just because your boss isn't doing his or her job doesn't mean you shouldn't be doing yours. At the same time, you should not simply tolerate your situation. Sometimes you have to ask for what you want. So, let your boss know that you would appreciate some recognition. If you find this uncomfortable, simply ask for feedback. For example, you could say, "Boss, I was hoping to get some feedback on the presentation that I gave yesterday." Don't be afraid to ask to be acknowledged or to have a positive e-mail forwarded to higher-ups in the organization. Beyond just making you feel respected, it is important for your own professional advancement to have your successes acknowledged and documented—especially if your boss were to leave the organization suddenly.

Whether or not you decide to tackle the issue of getting more recognition and feedback from your supervisor is your decision; however, doing so for your employees is your responsibility. As a supervisor, I suggest that you create a culture where asking to be acknowledged is perfectly acceptable. For example, you might say something like: "I want you to know that it is very important to me that each of you feel recognized and acknowledged for your contributions. In fact, it is my job to do so. If for any reason you feel that I'm not giving you the recognition or credit you deserve, please bring it to my attention. Can I count on you to do that?" By the way, as a supervisor, you'll earn a lot of respect by doing so.

8. **"I don't know how."** In truth, most people are not particularly skilled when it comes to using praise to reinforce behavior. I am always appreciative of people who recognize their limitations. Recognizing that you don't know how to do

something, however, doesn't relieve you of responsibility in learning how to do it. If this applies to you, fortunately, by the end of this chapter you will have the skills!

9. **"I never seem to catch the good behavior."** Managers or supervisors are generally quite good at identifying problematic behaviors but not nearly as good at recognizing employees' desirable behaviors. There is actually a simple explanation for this bias toward the bad and oversight of the good. Our brains have evolved to constantly scan our environment for behaviors and events that are out of the ordinary. If we come home and our door is wide open or the lights are on when they aren't supposed to be, we tend to notice.

In terms of supervising employees, no mental "red flags" pop up when we see employees working as they should. Imagine supervising an office staff of ten people. You come in one morning and see nine people at their desks working and one missing. Where does your attention go? Since good behavior does not elicit a natural prompt to get your attention, you must actually create physical prompts to remind you to catch desirable behavior until doing so becomes a habit. I've tried many different ways to help supervisors remember to praise good behavior. Here are the two that have worked the best. The first involves placing five pennies in your left pocket at the beginning of the work day. Each time you praise an employee, move a penny into the right pocket. You can't leave for the day without all the coins being moved over. The second strategy involves setting three alarms using either a program on your computer such as Outlook or a mobile device such as a cell phone or Blackberry. Set these alarms for midmorning, lunch, and midafternoon. Each time an alarm goes off, get up and start looking to catch and reinforce good behavior. I recommend that you *do not* rely on a sign or note on your desk as a reminder.

They are not powerful prompts that call us into action, and their novelty wears off quickly.

10. **"My employees never do anything worth praising them for."** Supervisors who think this way are either not paying enough attention to their employees or have the bar set unreasonably high. First, start spending more time working with your people and taking a more active interest in what they are doing. If you're really out of touch with your employees, you may have to ask them to tell you about their recent accomplishments. Second, lower your bar to a more reasonable level, perhaps not on everything but in a few areas that will allow your employees to achieve success. You don't have to let them know that you've lowered the bar; simply begin praising at lower levels of performance. Third, ask an employee to do something outside of his or her regular scope—keep it small and make it so he or she cannot help but succeed. In other words, set your employee up for success, giving you the ammo you need to praise him or her. Finally, ask others to share with you any good experiences they have with your team members. You can't benefit from the power of recognition if you never use it, and the longer you go without using it, the more disrespected and disengaged employees will feel. The good news is that regardless of your management style up to this point, employees nearly always respond positively to supervisors who make a sincere and concerted effort to recognize their work. Start today catching good behavior and taking responsibility for engaging your employees.

How to Praise Powerfully

Given that verbal praise, also called social reinforcement, is the single most effective form of recognition, it is important that you know how to deliver powerful praise. By *powerful* I mean praise that reinforces the behavior in a way that significantly increases the likelihood of that behavior occurring again in the future. In psychology, there is a whole lot we don't know, but one thing we know really, really well is how to deliver powerful praise and reinforce human behavior. There are four primary factors that determine the effectiveness of social reinforcement:

1. **Timing.** Deliver praise as quickly as possible after the desired behavior. Just imagine the difference between calling one of your employees at home to tell her what a great job she did on a presentation that afternoon versus mentioning it during her performance review a few months later.

2. **Specificity.** The goal of praise is to reinforce a specific behavior. Using general praise such as "Good job!" contributes very little to its effectiveness. Imagine someone saying, "You look nice today." You may feel good, but you don't know if it was the way you wore your hair, your shirt, your pants, or something else. Have you ever had your boss walk up and say, "Hey, you're really doing a good job" and honestly not know what she was talking about? Powerful praise looks like this: "Renée, I just want to commend you on how you handled that upset customer. You remained extremely professional and respectful. You listened and asked specific questions to fully understand the situation and apologized to the customer for the problem even though you had nothing to do in creating it. Really great job!" Now Renée knows what it was that you expect her to do more of next time—as might her team members who overheard your comments.

3. **Proximity.** One of the key factors uncovered by science that enhances the effectiveness of praise is physical proximity. The closer you are, the more impact it has. Imagine the difference between sending an e-mail to congratulate

someone on a job well done versus taking the time to physically walk to his or her office and say it in person. When you deliver praise personally you also have the opportunity to add nonverbal gestures for emphasis. Whenever possible, praise in person and accompany it with a handshake and smile.

4. **Enthusiasm.** We all know that how you say something is as important as what you say. The same applies here. Praising with energy and enthusiasm is more powerful than being stoic about it. I am not talking about getting out the pom-poms and doing a cheer (although that certainly would be memorable), but just know that the more enthusiastically you deliver your praise, the more impact it has. Regardless of your level of enthusiasm, it is critical that you deliver the feedback sincerely. Never leave your employees with even the slightest possible notion that you are being insincere.

Best Practices in Employee Recognition Awards

When it comes to leading people, David Bayes is about the smartest person I know. I met him during an assessment and development program I was conducting for team leaders. As much as I'm trained not to judge a book by its cover, I did just that with David. He is a "country boy" from the South who dropped out of school in the ninth grade to go to work and help his family. With his coarse physical appearance, thick country drawl, and phonetic writing, I didn't peg him as a great leader, but that's exactly what he is. In fact, he's probably the most effective team leader I've ever met. Through the years we've stayed in touch, and I always appreciate his real-world views and perspectives on leadership. While writing this chapter, I decided to ask David for his thoughts on how best to recognize employees. He shared with me the following example:

Let's say I ask John to come to my office. Everybody, including John, thinks he is in trouble because when we were kids we only got called to the principal's office for doing something bad. John comes into my office, and I ask him to sit down. I say, "Hi, John. How's it going?" He tells me. Then I say, "The reason I brought you in today is that you're doing a really great job and I wanted you to know that. I also wanted to hear if you have any ideas on how we could do things better." Wow—this will blow John away and make him feel good because it's personal and one-on-one. I'm asking for his ideas, and this shows him that I respect him. Taking the time to recognize your employees and ask for their ideas shows that you care and means more to them than anything. I got a plaque once for being a good supervisor, and it went right into the trash on the way home because I did not feel like they meant it.

David "gets it," and that's why his work crews consistently outperform those of other team leaders. In fact, employees ask to be moved to his shift. Recognizing employees and showing them respect isn't about plaques and gift cards; it's about something much more valuable—your sincere approval and your time. As human beings we are hard-wired to seek approval and acknowledgment from those we respect. Just as important, we seek to avoid disapproval. Have you ever had someone you really respected tell you that they were disappointed in you? It feels

The Yellow Sticky

Have you ever come back to your desk to find a yellow sticky with something like "Good Job!" written on it by your boss? Whenever I give a talk, I ask the audience this question. In an audience of a hundred people, usually two or three will raise their hand. I then ask them, "What did you do with it?" Only once have I had someone say that they threw it away. Every other person kept it visible in their work station, such as pasted on their computer monitor, for long periods of time. It's amazing that most of us get so little acknowledgment from our bosses that a yellow sticky with a few words takes on the significance of a prized trophy; a reminder that we did something worthy of recognition and thirty seconds of our boss's time. Employees may show up to work because of paychecks, but yellow sticky notes are far more valuable a currency when it comes to determining how hard they will work.

like a dagger, doesn't it? Employees exert extraordinary discretionary effort for David because of the mutual respect and desire for approval but also because they don't want to disappoint him.

It is really important to understand the powerful relationship between recognition and corrective feedback, namely, the greater the recognition, the more effective the feedback. Imagine having a highly critical supervisor who constantly points out your weaknesses and failings but never your strengths. Now, imagine having a supervisor who regularly acknowledges and recognizes you for your good work. Corrective feedback from which boss is more powerful? Obviously, it's the feedback from the one who regularly acknowledges you. Employees grow accustomed to constant negative feedback to the point that it becomes totally ineffective. In contrast, when we receive critical feedback within the context of mostly positive feedback, we take corrective action quickly. Thus, providing regular positive reinforcement not only increases positive behavior but also greatly enhances a supervisor's ability to deal powerfully with performance problems when they occur.

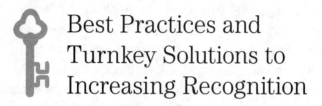

Best Practices and Turnkey Solutions to Increasing Recognition

As with each of the following chapters and RESPECT drivers, I have included very simple, tangible, effective, and low-cost strategies to increase employees' experience of being recognized in your organization. I encourage you to identify those that fit most comfortably with your personality and the culture of your organization and to begin implementing one today.

1. **Handwritten note.** Spend five dollars on a box of thank-you cards. Better yet, have your own note cards made up that say something like, "You Make a Difference." Keep them in your desk, and whenever employees exceed your expectations, send them a card thanking them for what they've done and what it has meant to you and the organization, team, or client. If you really want to go over the top, send the notes to employees' homes.

2. **Spread the word.** If one of your employees did something great, let people know, including announcing it at a departmental meeting and sending an e-mail to peers, your boss,

and even those higher up. If you want to give your employee a big boost of respect, have your boss or other upper management personally visit and congratulate your employee on a job well done.

3. **Make an example.** A great way to show respect is to use an employee's work as an example of excellence. For instance, a team member might have produced an exceptional report. At the next team meeting, share it and suggest that others use it as a template. Be careful not to imply that everyone else's work is terrible! You might say, for example, "Everyone on this team does good work—if you didn't you wouldn't be here. Sometimes somebody does something exceptional that we can all learn from. I am going to share such an example today so that our whole team can benefit."

4. **Give more say.** Recognize your employees' accomplishments by providing them with greater decision making and autonomy in their jobs. Let them and everyone on the team know that greater discretionary effort is rewarded with greater discretionary control over their job.

5. **Create more opportunities.** Employees who go above and beyond should be acknowledged with additional opportunities such as taking on new assignments or receiving specialized training. You need to send a message to your best employees that you value them and want to continue to support their growth and development.

6. **Wall of Great Ideas.** One company I work with honors its employees' best ideas by putting them on plaques and hanging them in the main lobby. The employees also receive a monetary award based on the impact of their suggestion. As you can imagine, employees take tremendous pride in seeing the plaques with their names and ideas hanging in the lobby, and it serves to inspire others to offer their suggestions.

7. **Document it!** Most employees get notes in their personnel folders for disciplinary action. The next time somebody does something noteworthy, put a note in his or her folder. This has a very practical advantage in that you are able to refer to it when completing performance reviews at the end of the year. It also has an extremely tangible and practical benefit to the employee and his or her career should you leave the company.

8. **Increased recognition.** Recognize an employee by giving him or her the opportunity for increased recognition. For example, you can have the employee either attend a meeting with you or go in your place where he or she will get exposed to higher-ups in the organization. If the employee is to play a role in the meeting, make sure that the employee is fully prepared so that he or she may achieve success.

9. **Meeting starter.** At the beginning of every team meeting ask people to go around the room and share one thing that an employee or fellow team member did that should be acknowledged. If the person being recognized is not in the room, encourage those present to pass along kudos when next they see the individual.

10. **Read all about it.** After your team finishes a big project, take out an ad in the local paper with everyone's name congratulating them on a job well done. People will love it!

The Bottom Line

Regardless of your philosophical beliefs about work ethic, the simple truth remains that acknowledging employees' contributions increases their sense of pride and respect, which in turn increases their discretionary effort and engagement. Employees whose efforts go unnoticed feel disrespected and disengage. There is no more basic or powerful tool in a supervisor's toolbox than positive reinforcement—and those who fail to use it are a liability, not an asset, to their organization. In the next chapter, we will look at another powerful tool for showing respect and engaging employees: empowerment.

CHAPTER 6 # Empowerment

> "The best executive is the one who has the
> sense enough to pick good men to do what he
> wants done, and self-restraint enough to keep
> from meddling with them while they do it."
>
> *—Theodore Roosevelt*

E mpowerment refers to providing your workforce with the training, resources, and opportunities they need to be successful. Leaders
empower employees through consistent information sharing
and increased decision-making responsibility and autonomy.
Those who empower employees encourage them to take educated risks, seek novel solutions, and treat mistakes as learning
opportunities. Supervisors also empower employees when they
take down roadblocks and eliminate processes that frustrate
team members and waste their time. Furthermore, they provide employees with a clear and consistent focus based on the
vision and mission of the organization. At the corporate level, a
company empowers its workforce by developing and adhering to
policies and procedures that facilitate productivity and creativity instead of impeding it.

We show respect to employees by creating fertile environments that allow them to flourish and to offer their full talents.
We not only disrespect employees when we cut off access to

information, training, resources, and learning opportunities, but we also limit their development as well as their ability to make a meaningful difference in the organization. Are you the kind of supervisor who creates an environment that maximizes the potential contributions of your employees or thwarts and frustrates their efforts? Take the following quiz to find out.

EMPOWERMENT SELF-ASSESSMENT QUIZ

Instructions: Read each statement below and decide how accurately it describes your behavior using the following scale:

- **a.** **Never or rarely engage in this behavior (0 points)**
- **b.** **Sometimes engage in this behavior (1 point)**
- **c.** **Regularly engage in this behavior (2 points)**
- **d.** **Always or almost always engage in this behavior (3 points)**

Place the point value of your answer choice on the blank line at the beginning of the statement.

_____ 1. **I regularly ask employees how I can help them be more successful.**

_____ 2. **I delegate as much decision-making responsibility as possible to employees.**

_____ 3. **I insist that employees receive continued training to expand their skills.**

_____ 4. **I actively encourage employees to take educated risks.**

_____ 5. **I ask employees for suggestions on eliminating or changing policies they find restrictive.**

_____ **Total Number of Points**

INTERPRETING YOUR SCORES

0-5: Your management approach is disrespectful, disempowering, and disengaging. You are actively limiting the potential of your employees and causing them significant frustration. Employees see you as holding them back and are likely to leave you and the organization unless you quickly and dramatically overhaul your management style.

6-10: While you do little to empower employees, you do not actively disempower them. With the overall goal of maximizing the human capital of your organization, you have a significant opportunity to provide learning and growth opportunities. You need to create an environment that will challenge and push your people to improve, not hamstring them.

11-15: Congratulations, your management style is one that maximizes the human capital of your organization by empowering employees to grow, develop, and deliver their best. Your people feel trusted and empowered to make decisions, experiment, and learn from their mistakes. Such employees will feel unencumbered by policies and procedures that limit their autonomy and create needless red tape. Your approach leads to employees feeling respected, empowered, and engaged.

Benefits to Having an Empowered Workforce

First and foremost, empowered employees have been sufficiently trained so that they are competent in their jobs. They do not look like the employees who accidentally hit a wrong button on the cash register and have to call their manager over to back them out of their mistake. Since they are competent, they are less likely to fail and less likely to quit. Naturally, well-trained, competent employees are more productive and more efficient than their disempowered counterparts.

The more empowered the employee, the more skilled, versatile, and valuable that person is to your organization. Cross-trained employees provide greater flexibility, as they have the ability to cover and support one another in different areas. Moreover, because empowered employees are competent and have been given greater autonomy and decision-making responsibility, they require less time and support from supervisors. Thus, empowered employees significantly add to an organization's human capital by not only being more highly skilled but also requiring fewer resources in terms of supervision.

Among the most important benefits of empowered employees is their ability to significantly improve processes. They are able to do this because their training in different job functions and increased access to information provides them with a big-picture perspective not available to less-educated and -trained employees. Because empowered employees feel respected and engaged, they take greater initiative, which further contributes to improved processes, services, and products. The combination of high skill, independence, big-picture perspective, and responsibility will make these employees among the most valuable in your organization.

Empowerment on the Playing Field

Given the benefits of having empowered employees on your team, it is quite astonishing how unempowered most employees are. For example, lack of training and limited opportunity for advancement are two of the leading reasons for turnover. What more basic way could we empower employees than to teach them what they need to know to be successful in their jobs? Yet, how often are employees thrown into their jobs and expected to instantly perform at a high level? We treat employees with respect when we set them up to succeed; in the same vein, we disrespect employees when we expect them to succeed in the absence of sufficient training. A friend's son, Steven, recently responded to a "Help Wanted" sign at a local retailer. At the end of a five-minute interview, Steven was asked how soon he could start. He said, "Right away," and was handed a company shirt and told to get out on the floor and start helping customers. After an hour he took off the shirt and went home.

Perhaps the example of Steven is extreme; however, rarely do employees receive initial training that prepares them even minimally to be successful in their roles. Rather, employees are often provided with the barest-bones training and expected to "pick it up" as they go. Even if employees possess the technical skills from previous work experience, they certainly have not performed their responsibilities within the context of the new organization and possibly within the industry. Once you've gone through the effort and expense of hiring a new team member, why wouldn't you do everything possible to make him or her successful? The resources required to train a new employee pale in comparison to the cost of lost productivity and expense of refilling the position.

Here are several reasons why you should be constantly growing and developing team members:

- Ongoing training communicates an expectation of continuous improvement as opposed to complacency.
- You demonstrate your trust and respect for employees as you show your confidence in their ability to take on added responsibility.
- As you increase employees' skills, you increase their value and hence the human capital of your organization.
- As employees are given new and challenging assignments, they become more engaged and invested.

Empowered employees are also less likely to become burned out or bored. Finally, continuous training and development fills the internal succession pipeline that, obviously, has a host of benefits including reduced costs of recruitment, greater acceptance by current team members, already established cultural fit, less chance of turnover, smoother transitions, and significantly less formal and informal training—you've already done most of it! There's one more benefit to promoting from within: increased respect and engagement by employees who see this as a show of commitment and respect by the organization toward current employees.

Examples of Empowerment

Quite simply, the more you invest in your employees the more valuable and engaged they become to your organization. The following examples are quotes from employees on the subject of empowerment. Consider what your employees might say if they were asked how they had been empowered in your organization:

- "When I was hired, my boss told me that it was his job to make me successful and whatever tools, training, or resources I needed, he would do his best to get. Although I haven't asked for much, whenever I have he has always come through. I feel that my boss respects me and really wants me to succeed."

- "I work for a package delivery business. I saw what I thought was an opportunity to save time by changing some routes based on new traffic patterns. I pitched it to my boss, and he said, 'What do you need from me?' I really appreciate the opportunity to work for a boss who actually values my ideas and encourages me to act on them."

- "My boss always tells us that she wants us to work like we own the company. She gives team members autonomy and decision-making authority. She says, 'If I didn't trust you to make decisions on your own, then I wouldn't have hired you.'"

- "I know most people hate training classes, but I love learning new skills. I have certain goals to meet, and whenever I meet those goals in a given quarter my supervisor lets me take another training course. This has led to a lot of opportunities for me and keeps me really engaged."

- "We got a new department manager about a year ago, and she immediately started having us cross-train. I can't tell you what a difference it has made for our team—both in terms of people getting along and in making improvements in our production process because employees know so much more about the different jobs and how they relate to each other."

- "I worked for a manager who had a philosophy of sharing information on a 'need-to-know-only' basis. Sometimes we heard about decisions our boss made from other employees who had heard it from their supervisor. Everyone felt totally in

continued

the dark, like he didn't trust or respect us. My current manager does everything she can to communicate and keep us in the loop. Her philosophy is to be totally open and transparent. Everyone really respects her because we feel like she respects us, and that translates into team members being more productive and happy at work."

• "Two of my co-workers and I had a novel idea for a new product. We pitched it to our boss, and he said, 'Go for it!' Even though our idea did not pan out, our boss really supported us and never made any of us feel bad about wasting time and money. In fact, despite the failure, he actually acknowledged us in front of the whole department for our initiative and creativity. I am proud to work for a boss who actually believes in and supports his people."

• "I started out with this company twenty years ago as an administrative assistant with a high school diploma. Now I have a graduate degree and am the assistant plant manager. This company believes in its people and believes in investing in them. I think that is why we have so little turnover and are as successful as we are."

• "I've worked as a customer service agent in a number of different retail stores. Most of the time they just throw you out onto the floor and you learn as you go. This company spent three weeks training me. They had me go around and work with two of the best team members. It is the first job that I ever felt really prepared and ready to do well, and also the first time that I really felt that the company cared."

• "I am an accountant, and I work for a major corporation. When I first got the job, everyone assumed that I knew what I was doing—but I was really struggling to learn the new system. After two weeks my boss called me in to see how I was doing, and I told him that I felt that I was in over my head. He immediately got me the training and support I needed to be successful. What really blew me away was that he apologized to me for not making sure that I was fully trained."

Best Practices and Turnkey Solutions to Empowering Employees

There are several low-cost, easy-to-implement strategies for empowering employees and increasing their value to the organization. The following list provides you with specific opportunities to get you started today.

1. **Improve new-hire training.** Hold meetings with your most recently hired employees and ask them for suggestions on how to improve the organization's onboarding and initial training processes and procedures.

2. **Ask your employees what they need to do their job more effectively.** Schedule individual meetings with your employees and ask them to tell you one thing that would make them more effective in their job. Often, these are minor requests but have a big impact on employees feeling respected

and empowered. If you cannot fulfill the request, let the employee know why and what you are able to do instead.

3. **Promote more cross-training.** Set a goal that each team member must be fully cross-trained in at least one other job in six months. Within obvious boundaries, allow employees to select the training.

4. **Brown-bag lunches.** Once a month, hold a brown-bag lunch and ask a leader from another department to come and share information with your team. For example, you might invite the CFO to come and give a thirty-minute overview of company financials and have him or her show how the numbers from your department impact the whole company.

5. **Create task forces to analyze processes and policies.** Ask for volunteers to form a subcommittee to review and make suggestions on eliminating or revising current policies and procedures that unnecessarily detract from employee productivity.

6. **Turn team members into coaches.** Foster a culture where employees coach and develop one another. Ask your human resources department to support your effort by holding a workshop to teach employees basic skills in giving constructive feedback. As the supervisor, make sure to recognize and acknowledge the team members who provide the greatest support to others. By the way, these are also the team members who should be identified as potential supervisors.

7. **Create learning opportunities.** Assign tasks to team members that serve as learning opportunities. Present employees with a menu of possible tasks and allow them to choose.

8. **Encourage autonomy.** Ask each employee to identify decisions that currently require approval by others and relinquish as much decision-making authority as possible.

The Bottom Line

The primary responsibility of supervisors or any leaders is to make those underneath them successful. We show respect for our employees when we provide them with the training and resources that lead to their success and ongoing development. As we challenge employees with new learning opportunities, they become increasingly more valuable and engaged, and they significantly increase the human capital of the organization. Reflect for a minute. Are you creating an environment in which employees can thrive or just survive? What suggestions and solutions can you take away from this chapter and begin implementing immediately to empower your employees?

Like empowerment, the next RESPECT driver is critically related to the continued growth, development, and success of employees: supportive feedback.

CHAPTER 7 Supportive
Feedback

"Truly great leaders spend as much time
collecting and acting upon feedback as they
do providing it."

—*Alexander Lucia, coauthor of*
Walk the Talk

G iving supportive feedback arms employees with
information to help focus, shape, and direct their
behavior. Whether positive or negative/corrective
in nature, all feedback should be delivered in a supportive manner. Supervisors must clearly communicate that their feedback
comes from a place of caring about the employee being successful—not only for the sake of the individual but also for the sake of
the team and larger organization. Keeping in mind that a supervisor's primary responsibility is to increase the human capital of
his or her organization, providing ongoing supportive feedback is
one of the most powerful tools in the managerial toolbox. Beyond
increasing the skills of their team members, supervisors demonstrate respect, commitment, and caring for their subordinates

when they offer ongoing constructive, encouraging, thoughtful, and sincere feedback every day.

The most effective supervisors take on the persona of a coach who provides training, mentoring, and feedback "in the moment" to his or her team members. Many great coaches have also been great players, but the traits, skills, and characteristics that make an individual a great coach are quite different from those that made him or her a successful player. Like the coach of an athletic team, successful supervisors have often been excellent employees; while having such a résumé provides credibility and practical technical support, it does not provide a background in knowing how to give specific, actionable, and timely feedback to employees. Like accomplished coaches, effective supervisors know how to deliver feedback to improve the performance of their team members. Do you pass the test of a good coach? Take the following quiz and find out.

SUPPORTIVE FEEDBACK SELF-ASSESSMENT QUIZ

Instructions: Read each statement below and decide how accurately it describes your behavior using the following scale:

   a. **Never or rarely engage in this behavior (0 points)**
   b. **Sometimes engage in this behavior (1 point)**
   c. **Regularly engage in this behavior (2 points)**
   d. **Always or almost always engage in this behavior (3 points)**

Place the point value of your answer choice on the blank line at the beginning of the statement.

_____ 1. **I give specific performance feedback to employees on a daily basis.**

_____ 2. **I always provide feedback in a supportive manner, even the most critical.**

_____ 3. **I encourage team members to provide me with regular feedback on my performance and effectiveness.**

_____ 4. **When I am concerned about an employee's behavior, I provide coaching within twenty-four hours of becoming aware of the problem.**

_____ 5. **I follow up with employees soon after giving corrective feedback to either reinforce the positive changes or provide continued coaching.**

_____ **Total Number of Points**

INTERPRETING YOUR SCORES

0-5: You are failing your employees and either need to immediately address this problem or go back to being a "player." Supervision is not for everyone. By not providing employees with regular feedback, you are not helping them to improve; in fact, the overall performance and effectiveness of the team will decrease as poor performance goes unchecked. Whether you realize it or not, your current lack of coaching or, as you may call it, "hands-off" approach is seriously limiting the potential of your team and overall human capital of your organization.

6-10: You are maintaining and may be slightly improving the overall skills and effectiveness of team members. However, your employees need more regular supportive feedback to really grow and develop. For individuals to realize their potential, they must be coached and mentored on a daily basis. Upping your game will significantly improve the performance and engagement of your team members.

11-15: Congratulations, you are an active and effective coach. You continuously seek to improve the skills of your team members and, in the process, demonstrate your respect for them and the value that they bring to the team. If you have not already begun doing so, start emphasizing the importance of both self-assessment and team-based feedback. Consider coaching other leaders in your organization who may be struggling in this area.

Benefits of Supportive Feedback

Providing ongoing supportive feedback lets employees know that you care about their performance and success. Imagine watching a high school athletic practice. Which kids get the most attention and feedback from the coach—the best players or the worst? Naturally, the best players get the most coaching because they are considered the most valuable part of the team. Being coached indicates respect for the team member and his or her skills. In contrast, players not seen as having much value or promise are given the least attention. The message to such team members is, "You don't really matter much" and "There isn't much hope for you." Naturally, such individuals feel disrespected, disenfranchised, and disengaged. Thus, by providing ongoing supportive feedback you demonstrate respect to team players and increase their level of engagement.

To effectively and efficiently develop team members and help them grow, supervisors must be skilled at providing feedback on a daily basis. The success and impact of any training program depends on the skill of the coach, teacher, or supervisor to provide supportive feedback while the task is actually being performed. In the absence of feedback, performance is likely to decline. Thus, the greatest benefit of ongoing supportive feedback is increased skills among team members, which increases their value to the organization.

From the perspective of learning and skill acquisition, ongoing coaching and feedback over time is far superior to training in bulk. For example, would you rather learn how to drive a race car in a single, four-hour session or in eight, thirty-minute sessions? Whether it is learning to race a car, balance a budget, or run a piece of equipment, distributed coaching sessions are far superior to onetime events. People are able to build their knowledge in steps. They are also able to practice skills between sessions, allowing them to develop questions that can be addressed during subsequent training. When supervisors provide regular feedback, they get to know the strengths and weaknesses of all employees and can make better decisions regarding how to best utilize their employees' talents. Supervisors are also in an educated position to know when to challenge employees to take on additional responsibilities.

Providing regular feedback to employees also means that you are in the game with them and you know when something is not working well. Dealing with problems when they first arise obviously requires and wastes fewer resources than when issues go unidentified and unchecked. It is also much easier, less awkward, and more effective to discuss problem behaviors with employees when they are new rather than long-standing. Hence, providing ongoing feedback to employees saves organizational resources by nipping problems in the bud. Whether you are a supervisor or baseball coach, the model is the same, namely, provide your players with up-front training and practice, send them into the game, and give them ongoing feedback.

Story from the Trenches

Tom had worked as a plant manager for five years and was just getting ready to receive his first performance review. Andrew, Tom's boss and the company president, asked me to facilitate. I met with Tom and reviewed his self-assessment prior to the meeting. Unfortunately, Andrew did not complete his assessment of Tom in advance; in fact, he was just finishing it as I arrived. Although Tom was already waiting, I asked that we delay the meeting for a few minutes so that I could review Andrew's assessment. After scanning his answers, I apologized and said that something had just come up and we needed to reschedule.

A few minutes after Tom left, I called Andrew and asked if his intention was for Tom to quit. Andrew said, "Of course not; he is one of my best plant managers." I told him that I had called the meeting off because that is most likely what would happen if I allowed the meeting to continue. I went on to explain that while Tom's self-evaluation was nearly all positive, Andrew's evaluation of Tom was nearly all negative. I asked Andrew why he would give one of his best plant managers such an awful review. He responded that Tom's numbers had been down lately and he wanted to give him a wake-up call.

I asked Andrew, "If you worked for someone and had not gotten a performance review in five years, how would you think you were doing?" He responded, "I guess I would think that I was doing pretty well." Correct. I told Andrew that *he* actually deserved the low performance evaluation and wake-up call. Not only would it be unfair to punish Tom because he had a lousy supervisor, but I could guarantee that after reading the review Tom would become so upset that he would disengage and most likely start looking for work elsewhere. In light of our conversation, I asked Andrew to reconsider his evaluation. Begrudgingly, he raised a few of the lowest scores.

When we reconvened the following week, Tom sat quietly reading his review. When he finished, he looked up at Andrew and said, "I cannot believe that in the five years that I have worked for you that you did not respect me enough to tell me that I wasn't meeting your expectations." Tom was hurt and angry, and he had a right to be. He told Andrew that he didn't see much point in working for someone whom he had obviously been failing for such a long time. It took a pay raise and six months to get Tom back in the game. If you respect your employees, you will give them regular feedback; you won't leave them assuming or guessing how they are doing. As you look at your team roster, do you have players who haven't received the kind of supportive feedback they need from you to continue improving? Begin a dialogue today, and don't wait for a performance review.

The Dreaded Performance Review

Most organizations would be well advised to throw out and discontinue their performance review forms and processes. The fact that supervisors and employees uniformly *hate* the performance review process should tell us that something isn't working right. The pain associated with the review process comes from supervisors not having provided employees with ongoing feedback throughout the year. Supervisors often use the performance review process as the time to deliver all the bad news at once. Could you imagine a football coach waiting until season's end to give his players feedback on all of the things they could have done better throughout the season? As absurd, unproductive, and ineffective as such an approach sounds, it is exactly how most supervisors feel about and conduct the performance review. Let me suggest that if supervisors deliver even one piece of surprising critical feedback during a performance review, they are not doing their job.

In truth, the performance review should be an opportunity to celebrate the accomplishments of the past year and serve as a personal development and goal-setting session. It should be a time to think about big-picture issues and reflect on what the employee learned in the prior year and how he or she can apply it going forward. The review should include a conversation about how effective the supervisor was in supporting and facilitating the employee's development and how he or she can be more effective going forward. Supervisor and employee should leave the review feeling energized and enthusiastic, not as though they had just come from a root canal.

Fundamentals of Supportive Feedback

Unfortunately, most supervisors are not trained in how to most effectively provide ongoing supportive feedback to their employees; they also rarely have good role models. Here are some fundamentals to get you started. The first and most important thing to remember is that the feedback is coming from a place of caring about the employee and his or her success. It is not about whether the feedback is positive or critical. All feedback should simply be considered supportive. If we care about people, we give them feedback even though it might be embarrassing. On several occasions I have been asked by CEOs to tell an executive that he or she had bad breath, had body odor, or invaded others' personal space. Without exception, the person appreciated the feedback and was upset that no one told him or her sooner. Have you ever had an undone button or zipper and no one told you? Wouldn't you have appreciated hearing about it?

Second, let your team members know that you have set a goal to give more feedback "in the moment"—don't start doing it out of the blue. Tell employees that you realize how much more helpful you find feedback when it is relevant and fresh as compared to appearing months later during a performance evaluation. Let them know that if the feedback is at all corrective in nature, you will be giving it in private. Emphasize that your goal is to provide feedback that is helpful—just like any coach would do for his team members. Encourage employees to provide you with regular feedback, and thank those who do so.

Third, when you begin giving feedback, keep it mostly positive and very short. For example, "Jim, I just wanted to let you know what a nice job I thought you did on that e-mail newsletter," "Carmen, that was an excellent point you made in the meeting this morning," and "Greg, good catch yesterday with that missing invoice." You want to practice and get comfortable using positive feedback. As discussed in Chapter 5, "Recognition," you want to be as specific as possible with your feedback.

After a few weeks, begin looking for opportunities to offer some light suggestions to employees. For example, "Tom, I noticed that you had a tough time getting your point across in that meeting. Can I offer a suggestion? [Wait for employee to respond affirmatively.] I think it would have been more powerful and probably helped your cause if you had turned the numbers into a bar chart and graphed the data over the past few quarters to put things in perspective." Such an approach will come across as supportive and helpful and may well lead to a longer conversation and deeper coaching opportunity. As you get more comfortable and skilled, you can choose larger, more significant issues about which to give feedback.

On average, 75 to 85 percent of your feedback should be positive and oriented toward reinforcing behavior, while 15 to 25 percent should be concerned with improving performance. My suggestion is that you never mix feedback. Some supervisors like to do the "feedback sandwich," that is, one slice positive feedback, one slice corrective feedback, and then one final slice positive feedback. The rationale is that the employee will be more receptive to corrective feedback after hearing a compliment and will leave on a positive note after receiving the second bit of good feedback. There are two significant problems with this approach. First, the corrective feedback is diluted by the adjacent positive feedback and often lost entirely—the employee remembers only the positive. Second, if the feedback sandwich is your *modus operandi* for delivering critical feedback, the positive feedback will come across as insincere. As soon as you start praising the employee, he or she will think, "OK, just get to the issue you're upset about." If the purpose of the feedback is to reinforce good behavior, keep it positive. If the purpose is to address a performance problem, keep it corrective. Your feedback will come across as more sincere and will be more effective in both situations.

Whatever your current skill level in delivering feedback, know there is always room for improvement. As you read over the examples that follow, highlight those that would lead most quickly to an increase in your effectiveness.

Examples of Supportive Feedback

- "At my company, we have 'coaching moments.' Whenever a supervisor wants to give feedback to an employee—positive or critical—the supervisor pulls the employee aside right away and gives the feedback."
- "Our supervisor compares herself to a basketball coach and calls us her star players. She emphasizes the importance of ongoing communication and feedback so we can improve both as individuals and as team members."
- "Our supervisor had us go through training on how to give feedback to one another. Because of it, we are all better communicators and work much more effectively as a team."
- "We got a new supervisor, and he spends part of each shift on the line watching us work, asking us questions, and making suggestions. He never yells or screams like our last supervisor, and if he wants you to do something different he'll just say, 'Why don't you try it this way?' He's always helping us to get better but never makes us feel stupid or bad—even when we make mistakes."
- "At the beginning of every shift we spend five to ten minutes talking about how the work went the day before and what we might have done differently to have been more effective. Our supervisor is there, but he mostly lets us do the talking."
- "Our supervisor regularly asks us to give him feedback about how he is doing. No matter what we say he never disputes it or becomes defensive. He listens, makes sure that he understands, and then asks for advice on how he can do better going forward.

continued

If he screwed up, he apologizes. Needless to say, we all have tremendous respect for him and are very receptive when he gives us feedback."

- "Friday afternoons our supervisor meets for five minutes with all twenty team members individually. She uses this time to give us feedback, ask for our feedback, and ask what she can do to make next week better for us."

- "I'm in customer service, and we get a lot of angry people that show up at our desk. Our supervisor is always trying to coach us and help us improve. Right after a particularly difficult customer, she asks us how it went and what we could have done to make it go better. The best thing she does is role-play with us to help us practice for the next time we are in such a situation. It's way more helpful than any training class I have ever been to."

Best Practices and Turnkey Strategies for Supportive Feedback

The following section provides specific, pragmatic, and actionable strategies to increase the effectiveness of your feedback efforts. They are intended to work for supervisors with different circumstances and levels of experience. Read through them and select two or three that you want to start using immediately.

1. **Focus on behavior.** Always focus the feedback on the impact or consequences of the behavior; never make it about the person. Also, *never* tell people they have a "bad attitude"—if you do, you'll really get a bad attitude! Make sure to identify the specific behavior that you want, and explain the importance and value of engaging in this behavior.

2. **Schedule your feedback.** To both prompt yourself and be more efficient, schedule your feedback on your calendar at the beginning of the week. Consider not just your own schedule but others' as well. When is the best time for your employees?

3. **In the moment.** Use the idea of "coaching moments" to give employees feedback as quickly as possible after a given situation. The fresher the feedback the more helpful.

4. **Role-play.** Verbal feedback should be supplemented with role-playing. Discuss the situation, have the team member decide on a different strategy, and then role-play it with him or her to see how it goes. Ideally, you would videotape and then review the role-play with the employee; it is by far the most powerful and effective training technique.

5. **Frequency.** A supervisor should spend a minimum of 5 percent of his or her day engaged in a feedback conversation, or roughly twenty-four minutes in eight hours.

6. **Batch your feedback.** If you are going to spend twenty-four minutes a day giving feedback, break it up into three eight-minute or two twelve-minute periods.

7. **Focused feedback.** You can give people feedback on anything and everything. To make your feedback maximally effective, focus it. For example, the feedback could be focused on the tasks that are most important to the employee's job or the area in which the employee is having the greatest difficulty.

Or, you might pick a feedback theme where for a given month all feedback is focused on a particular area such as customer service. Another approach is to give feedback in the area in which the employee has taken the most pride or interest in becoming exceptional. Instead of guessing, ask the employee if there is a particular area in which he or she would like feedback; this will also make the employee feel respected.

8. **Role model.** Serve as a role model to your employees by encouraging them to give you feedback. If it is not part of your culture, you will need to introduce it by setting time aside in a meeting and specifically requesting feedback. If you ask for feedback and no one speaks, then ask for feedback in a specific area about which you know people have particular concerns or interests. Also, you should meet with employees one-on-one for their feedback, particularly those who are more introverted and less likely to speak up in group meetings.

9. **Peer feedback.** Just as in sports, feedback from one team member to another can be especially powerful—even more powerful than feedback from the coach. Getting team members to provide one another with feedback is not going to happen naturally if it is not part of your culture. Consider speaking with your team about the idea and get their thoughts. Suggest bringing in a communications expert who can provide feedback training. Make sure that employees know this is all about supporting one another and not about criticizing fellow team members. If you see any team members giving abusive feedback, you must deal with it immediately.

10. **Feedback Friday.** Every Friday, meet for a few minutes with each of your team members individually. During this time give employees any feedback that you may not have had

time to give during the week. And make sure to highlight the best of their work. Ask them if they have any feedback for you and also how you can help them be more successful going forward.

The Bottom Line

As a manager, growing and developing employees so that they remain engaged and continue to become more valuable to the organization is your primary and most important responsibility. Providing regular, supportive feedback to all employees as a sports coach would to his players is a critical part of the process. The next driver in the RESPECT Model—partnering—takes this coach-player relationship to the next level.

CHAPTER 8 # Partnering

> "In the past a leader was a boss. Today's
> leaders must be partners with their people."
>
> —*Ken Blanchard*

The concept of partnering transcends teamwork and implies a degree of autonomy, discretion, equality, openness, power, and ownership that blurs traditional management-employee boundaries. Partners are not simply loyal team members; they are co-stewards of the organization's mission and vision, and they must readily take responsibility for its vitality. Building collaborative working relationships with employees creates the ultimate engaged employee—the employee who treats the business as though he or she owns it. In addition to partnerships among team members and their supervisor, such relations can bridge across departments and functional business units that readily share their resources and create synergies. The real power of an organization exists in fostering partnerships among employees at all levels.

Organizations also form external partnerships with customers, vendors, unions, government agencies, industry associations, and more. Such alliances provide additional resources, enhanced opportunities, and increased stability. Leaders who develop and foster mutually advantageous internal and external partnerships add considerable value to their organization. Are you such a leader? The following self-assessment will help you answer that question.

PARTNERING SELF-ASSESSMENT QUIZ

Instructions: Read each statement below and decide how accurately it describes your efforts at partnership using the following scale:

a. **Never or rarely engage in this behavior (0 points)**
b. **Sometimes engage in this behavior (1 point)**
c. **Regularly engage in this behavior (2 points)**
d. **Always or almost always engage in this behavior (3 points)**

Place the point value of your answer choice on the blank line at the beginning of the statement.

_____ 1. **I give team members authority and responsibility for making most decisions.**

_____ 2. **I openly share financial and big-picture information with employees.**

_____ 3. **I actively share information and resources with other departments.**

_____ 4. **I actively involve employees in hiring decisions.**

_____ 5. **I regularly reach out to internal and external customers for feedback.**

_____ **Total Number of Points**

INTERPRETING YOUR SCORES

0-5: You maintain a traditional management-employee hierarchy that does not show respect for your employees' ideas or abilities. Employees are unlikely to feel engaged in their work or relationship to you. There is little synergy within your department or with other departments. Your behaviors actively suppress a sense of partnership and greatly limit the potential of your people and team.

6-10: Your behaviors support teamwork but not partnering. Employees will experience some level of respect and engagement. Collaboration may exist among some team members but is unlikely to occur across departments. There is an opportunity for you to show greater respect to employees and engage them more fully in partnership.

11-15: Your leadership style demonstrates great respect for employees and fosters meaningful and effective partnerships. Your employees are likely to feel highly engaged and will more readily reach out and partner with both internal and external customers. Continue to look for opportunities to strengthen and expand your alliances with your team members, other departments, and those outside your organization.

Benefits of Partnering

The most obvious benefit of partnering is the synergy created through combined resources, skills, and abilities to achieve goals not otherwise attainable. As Stephen Covey suggests in his book *Principle-Centered Leadership*: "The basic role of the leader is to foster mutual respect and build a complementary team where each strength is made productive and each weakness made irrelevant." When employees can focus on their strengths, the organization benefits from increased productivity and higher-quality work. At the organizational level, successful partnerships may lead to increased revenue streams, lower production costs, and improved distribution channels.

Partnerships focus efforts toward a common goal. In so doing, team members are more likely to perform at a higher level for the sake of the mission and vision of the organization, rather than just worrying about looking good. In the words of Robert Yates, "It is amazing what can be accomplished when nobody cares about who gets the credit." Partners are willing to negotiate and sacrifice individual glory to further the overall goals of the partnership. They also feel significant responsibility toward one another and ownership toward the organization. Such individuals are much more likely to take pride in their work, which translates into higher levels of quality.

Partners continually provide one another with ongoing supportive feedback, as discussed in the previous chapter. They do so out of respect for one another and because of their interest in achieving common goals. Thus, partners become each other's best coaches and push one another to excel. When one partner improves, the overall skill level of the partnership increases. There is no substitute for having partners who "have your back." In a culture of partnering, individuals watch out for one another and assist as needed. This kind of support reduces individual stress and leads to greater overall productivity.

The difference in the productivity and efficiency of a team managed by a supervisor who has promoted partnership versus a traditional supervisor-employee relationship is astounding. Since they have more autonomy and decision-making responsibility, employees are able to make decisions without having to stop and wait for direction or approval. For example, imagine an assembly line going down. In one case, partnered employees quickly begin problem solving and brainstorming solutions, while traditionally managed employees are content to stop and wait for direction from their supervisor even when they know what should be done. Moreover, employees actually engaged in doing the work and using the equipment are often the ones most qualified to make the best decision. Waiting for supervisors to make or approve decisions that the employee is readily capable of making is not only unproductive and inefficient but also highly disrespectful and will likely foster disengagement.

Fundamentals of Partnering

Supervisors interested in creating partnerships with and among team members must start by fostering teamwork and collaboration. To quote Marvin Weisbord, "Teamwork is the quintessential contradiction of a society grounded in individual achievement." Although we may speak of the importance of teamwork both in business and in sports, rarely is it the supportive team member who receives the accolades. To foster teamwork, a supervisor must emphasize that no one wins unless everyone wins. There must be a continuous emphasis on employees working collaboratively toward a common goal, and employees should know precisely how their work contributes to that goal. You should reinforce group efforts and not individual accomplishments. It should be the employee who puts aside his or her work to help another who receives recognition.

Like teamwork, successful partnering at any level requires clearly defined roles and goals, open communication, trust, respect, and adherence to a common mission and vision. Supervisors partner with employees by actively eliciting their suggestions, creating flexibility and autonomy in their jobs, and extending to them decision-making authority. Partnering also requires openly sharing big-picture information, including the financials of the organization; fostering this kind of egalitarian culture leads to employees feeling highly respected, empowered, and engaged. Employees will demonstrate high levels of initiative and discretionary effort and begin thinking of themselves more as business partners than employees.

Successful partnering requires both empowering employees and providing them with ongoing supportive feedback as already discussed. Supervisors must demonstrate their commitment to their employees' growth and success by providing new learning opportunities and challenging assignments. They take the time to get to know their employees' personal and professional ambitions and offer guidance, coaching, and mentoring. Partnering supervisors let their employees know that they believe in them and support them. They also treat their employees as colleagues, not as subordinates, and take pleasure in highlighting their accomplishments so that they may be recognized by the organization.

Partnering occurs across departments when employees have the opportunity to work together on special projects in cross-departmental teams. All too often, departments fail to benefit from one another's resources and, as a result, tend to engage in redundant efforts. Moreover, solutions reached by individual departments looking at issues from only their perspective are rarely as beneficial as those reached through interdepartment collaboration. Likewise, team members working independently—or even at cross-efforts—will never realize the synergy that can be reached through active partnership.

Successful organizations also seek to develop collaborative relationships with their customers, vendors, and other external organizations. Care should be taken to regularly reach out and meet with external partners to identify additional opportunities and benefits. Many organizations fail to consider the importance of engaging their vendors and customers as business partners who, just like engaged employees, will help solve problems, create new products and services, ask insightful questions, and provide input that leads to improvements. As I examine my own business relationships both as a vendor and as a customer, I realize how much more committed and engaged I am to those individuals and organizations who treat me as a valued business partner.

Supervisors and organizations have innumerable avenues to foster internal and external partnerships. Below are various real-world examples that I hope will prove useful in furthering your own partnerships.

Examples of Partnering

- "Sometimes we are shorthanded. Instead of shutting the whole line down for breaks, our supervisor fills in. I appreciate a boss who is willing to roll up his sleeves up and get dirty."
- "Once a quarter, we have what is called 'Trading Places' at our company. For half the day we work with someone else from another department, and then for the other half day they work with us. It is our favorite day of the month, and it has had

continued

an extremely positive impact on departments collaborating with each other."

• "I work on a production team in a manufacturing company. Every year our boss involves us in the budget process and in making requests for new equipment. When we get the opportunity to buy new equipment we do the research, meet with the salespeople, and make the decision. It makes so much sense to have the people who are actually using the equipment decide on it!"

• "The sales and marketing departments were always pointing fingers at each other and never seemed to be on the same page. The department managers decided to go to one another's meetings and bring along a team member. It has really helped communication between the teams, and we are now much more on the same page."

• "The president of our company says that we are all business partners together and that his job is no more important than anyone else's. He regularly goes around to different departments and spends time working with employees at every level. The other day he answered the main switchboard number, and one night last year he came in and emptied trash with the cleaning crew! Everyone in this company has so much respect for him."

• "Our company produces flooring, and we sell to large chain stores around the country. When a customer has a problem, one of the hourly employees actually goes with the salesperson to personally visit that customer—sometimes it means flying across the country. I think this is a great idea because the guys who actually make the flooring get to speak directly with the customers. It also shows a lot of respect for the hourly guys."

• "I work for a family-owned business of about 250 employees. Once a quarter we all meet, and the president goes through all the numbers with us and lets us know exactly how the company is doing and asks us how we can do better. He treats us like business partners and not just employees."

• "We used to get sales and commission reports from accounting that we just couldn't understand. We used to complain to our boss, but she never did anything. We got a new boss, and as soon as we brought it up he had someone from accounting come to our team meeting to talk with us. We ended up making several suggestions and improving the report both for us and for accounting."

• "We consider our vendors and customers our business partners. Each year we hold a big one-day event where we invite them to participate in various meetings, get their feedback, and brainstorm about new products and services."

• "Our organization has a cross-department team that meets monthly to brainstorm on how we can better support and collaborate with one another. This process has led to numerous improvements and opportunities, as well as a much increased sense of partnership across the organization."

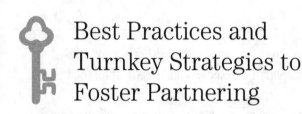

Best Practices and Turnkey Strategies to Foster Partnering

Fostering a culture of partnering in your organization requires communication and creativity. The following list describes several ways to make your employees feel like valuable partners.

1. **Benefits.** If you're going to treat your employees like partners, then everyone should have the same benefits. For example, the CEO and janitors at Nucor Steel have the same benefits package, and the executives don't have perks such as company cars or preferred parking spaces. If you have preferred parking spaces for upper management, get rid of them—they are daily reminders to employees and visitors of a culture that devalues its employees.

2. **Department representative.** Each month choose a team member to represent your department at a monthly meeting of all departments. During the meeting, representatives from each department provide a monthly update, share best practices, and look for opportunities to share resources and partner with one another.

3. **Finance meeting.** Every quarter provide employees with full financial disclosure. Make sure the information is presented in a manner that allows those less familiar with accounting practices to understand the numbers; offer interested employees basic training in reading financial statements.

4. **Employee owned.** If possible, employees should be stockholders of the company. Ideally, compensation should be tied directly to individual, team, and corporate performance.

5. **State of the Union.** CEOs should regularly update employees on major business issues. Depending on the company's size and technological sophistication, the presentation can be streamed over the company intranet and recorded as a video and audio podcast. Ideally, the CEO would also entertain questions. At a minimum, the CEO should send out a company-wide weekly e-mail or hardcopy news update.

6. **You know what I know.** As a leader in your organization nothing communicates partnering more than keeping an open flow of information to your employees. Never leave your employees wondering if you are withholding information. *Keeping employees well informed will keep them well engaged.*

7. **Drumbeat meeting.** Every morning, team members gather and give a quick update of their work plan for the day. The meeting should also be used to ask questions, clarify issues from the day before or that day, and request assistance. To expedite the meeting, people should remain standing.

8. **Self-development.** Employees should be responsible for creating and executing their development plans. Supervisors should provide resources, support, and guidance; however, the employees should be the ones to drive their development and be held accountable.

9. **Cross-training.** The best way to foster partnering within your department is to cross-train people so that they know one another's jobs and can support one another. Each employee should be sufficiently qualified to cover two other positions for a period of at least two weeks.

10. **Department swap.** To foster partnering among departments, regularly have employees spend time learning about and cross-training in different departments. Also, department meetings should include team members from other

departments, which will promote communication and understanding as well as provide departments with additional perspectives and ideas.

11. **Partner audit.** How good a partner are you to your internal and external business partners? Create a brief survey and have team members meet with and interview your partners, including other departments, customers, and vendors, to see how you're doing and how you can improve.

12. **Mentor program.** All employees should have mentors one level above them from a different department. Employees and mentors should meet at least once per month for thirty minutes. Conversations should remain confidential. Begin by finding a mentor for yourself, and then ask others you know in the organization to mentor your employees. This program also shows respect to the mentors by asking them to participate.

13. **Team input.** Team members and supervisors should work together to make any major decisions in the department, including new equipment purchases, creating the budget, and hiring new team members.

14. **Employee council.** Create an employee council with as heterogeneous a mix of employees as possible based on department, position, age, ethnicity, gender, education, tenure, and so forth. The council should meet monthly with members of the executive team to share concerns, provide input, ask questions, and make requests.

15. **Blog.** Incorporate department blogs on the employee intranet. Blogs should be updated daily and provide real-time headline news on current business issues. Employees should also be able to post their thoughts and pose questions. The more organizations communicate with their employees, the more their employees will engage.

The Bottom Line

Do you make your employees feel like valued partners? Do you respect their input or go about making decisions without engaging your own internal experts? When we respect people, we treat them as equals and partners. In so doing, you will dramatically increase their performance and productivity. There is another way to almost instantly and dramatically increase your human capital, namely, by setting clear expectations and holding employees accountable for meeting those expectations, and it is the subject of the next chapter.

CHAPTER 9 Expectations

"High expectations are the key to everything."
—*Sam Walton*

The most common reason that employees fail to meet performance expectations is that those expectations were never made clear in the first place. Similar to giving feedback, supervisors consistently over-rate the degree to which they provide clear, specific goals to employees. Supervisors who get frustrated with employees for not performing as expected have often failed to set clear expectations. In addition to clearly defined goals, you must ensure that employees have the sufficient tools, training, and resources, including information and time, to successfully meet expectations.

During high school, I worked part-time as a night janitor at a local 3M plant. Although cleaning offices isn't particularly complicated or difficult work, like any new task, there is a learning curve. The first week I really struggled, but by the end of the second week I was starting to feel competent, and by the end of the third I felt like a pro. It was at this point that my supervisor told me that if I didn't start doing a better job, he would have to let me go. It turned out that I was cleaning only two-thirds of what I was expected to be cleaning in a full shift. He told me that he started employees off slowly so that they could catch on, but I clearly wasn't getting any quicker. Of course, he never communicated this approach to me up front. He then showed me the new areas to be cleaned, and the very next day I finished all with time to spare. Tasks take the time you give them, and people work to the goals you set. Do your employees clearly know your expectations?

Setting challenging goals that support the organization's mission and vision is a critical part of your job as you seek to maximize your human resources. At the same time, supervisors must make sure that employees' expectations are being met. For example, what do your employees expect in terms of development and advancement opportunities? While an employee may be meeting the expectations of his supervisor, if his own goals and expectations are not being met, he will likely become discouraged and disengaged. How effective are you at developing and managing the goals and expectations of team members? Take the following self-assessment and find out.

EXPECTATION MANAGEMENT SELF-ASSESSMENT QUIZ

Read each statement below and decide how accurately it describes your management style using the following scale:

a. **Never or rarely engage in this behavior (0 points)**
b. **Sometimes engage in this behavior (1 point)**

c. **Regularly engage in this behavior (2 points)**
d. **Always or almost always engage in this behavior (3 points)**

Place the point value of your answer choice on the blank line at the beginning of the statement.

_____ 1. **I set expectations and goals in collaboration with my employees.**

_____ 2. **I make sure that goals include measurable outcomes and time frames.**

_____ 3. **I explain the *why* behind the expectations.**

_____ 4. **When employees fail to meet goals or expectations, I look first at my own behavior to see where I could have let my employee down.**

_____ 5. **I hold employees accountable to meeting their performance goals.**

_____ **Total Number of Points**

INTERPRETING YOUR SCORES

0-5: Your employees feel very disconnected from you and the goals that are set for them. They feel disrespected and are at risk of disengaging. Your supervisory style is significantly reducing the productivity and efficiency of your department. Begin improving your skills in this area immediately. In addition to the suggestions in this chapter, consider identifying a mentor skilled in this area who could offer advice and guidance toward your development.

6-10: Employees are somewhat engaged and connected to their goals. Your modest skills in collaboratively setting clear expectations and holding employees accountable will result in acceptable but not superior levels of performance. By following the suggestions in this chapter you will significantly move the needle on your employees' success in meeting their goals as well as their level of engagement.

11-15: Your supervisory style sets your employees up for success in meeting their goals and leads them to a sense of accomplishment and pride. Continue to engage employees and work toward them taking full responsibility for setting their own goals. Encourage team members to hold one another accountable for reaching their goals. Consider serving as a mentor to supervisors in your organization who may have difficulty in this area.

Benefits of Setting Clear Expectations and Goals

The most obvious and important benefit of setting clear goals and expectations is that you are more likely to get the outcome you desire. If my wife tells me, "Bring something home for dinner" and I show up with a pizza and she's disappointed, she doesn't have much room to complain. The more specific one is in making a request, the more likely that request is to be met. Successful accomplishment of the goal leads to a feeling of achievement and an increased sense of pride and satisfaction. In addition, "getting it right" leads to quality and efficiency. When goals and objectives are clear, we don't have to worry about timely and expensive rework or producing work that is not quite on target. When employees know precisely what is expected, they do not waste time guessing or going off-course. Giving clear directions around a task has the same benefits as giving clear driving instructions; they allow you to get where you're going directly with little ambiguity. Think of a time when you had vague directions and wondered, "Was I supposed to turn there?" It is a frustrating and time-wasting experience; giving unclear instructions to your employees has the same impact.

By setting clear expectations with employees, you also help team members prioritize their work so that resources and efforts are properly apportioned. Have you ever had a supervisor pile one task on top of another without distinguishing their relative importance? This is more than simply frustrating; it leads to inefficiency and poor-quality work because employees may end up rushing important tasks—and this impacts others who may be waiting on the work to be completed. To ensure that your people are properly spending their most scarce resource—time—make sure that their tasks are clearly prioritized and that they have the tools necessary to successfully complete each task.

When expectations are clear, employees can be properly recognized and acknowledged for meeting and exceeding those expectations. Just as important, those who do not meet goals can be readily held accountable. High-performing employees become highly demoralized when no distinction is made between their contributions and those of poor performers. When expectations and goals are vague, such as, "Just do your best," it becomes much more difficult for employees to know what to do and for supervisors to evaluate employees fairly. In the world of performance management, vague goals and expectations lead to all kinds of difficulties.

Finally, setting clear expectations leads to employee satisfaction and engagement. For example, newly hired employees hold certain expectations based on their interviews. When those expectations are clear and fulfilled, employees are naturally satisfied. When expectations are vague, however, new employees tend to be overly optimistic and content with their performance relative to their supervisor's expectations. When informed that their performance has missed the mark, employees become demoralized and frustrated because the mark was not clear. In addition, when expectations are clear and the reasons behind them made explicit, employees experience higher levels of engagement as they see how their work contributes to fulfilling the mission and vision of the organization. Making sure that expectations fit with the overall strategic plan is a fundamental principle in setting effective goals and leads into our next section.

Expectation and Goal-Setting Fundamentals

Supervisors should always believe that their employees want to meet goals and expectations. Except for the highly disengaged, employees want to "get it right," and when they don't, you should assume that it is due to miscommunication or insufficient resources rather than apathy, laziness, or stupidity. People don't like to fail; we're just not wired that way. Ask yourself, when was the last time that you either purposely failed or felt good about failing? Why, then, would you assume that others feel differently? Here's the truth: if your employees are failing to meet expectations and goals, it is because you have failed them. Your job is to make your people successful, and you have to take responsibility for setting them up for success. If you believe that the primary reason that people fail to meet goals has to do more with them than you, then you should not be in the business of supervising, developing, or leading people.

Setting clear expectations begins during the interview process as hiring managers let employees know what they can expect and what will be expected of them. For example, if the culture of the organization is such that employees come in early and work late, you better make sure to mention that during the interview. When employees feel as though they have not been told the whole truth about the job, they feel disrespected and begin to disengage immediately. You should be clear regarding issues around training, resources, support, growth opportunities, and so on. Employees should also be clearly informed of what challenges they can expect to meet and what not to expect. For example, if a supervisor expects that a new hire will hit the ground running with little training, feedback, or support, then he or she should make that clear. If the potential employee's opportunity to advance in the organization will be limited by the lack of a college degree, that should be mentioned during the interview. The more clear and transparent the expectations are during the hiring process, the greater the satisfaction of both employee and manager.

How to Effectively Set Goals and Communicate Expectations

To achieve maximum effectiveness, goals should be clearly defined, meaningful, challenging, achievable, and time-limited. Tying goals to actual data is critical. For example, setting a goal of increasing quarterly sales by 5 percent will almost always yield higher performance than simply creating a goal of increasing sales with no set target. Goals provide focus, and reaching them provides a sense of accomplishment and pride. Without clear goals, efforts are often uncoordinated. Collaborating with employees while setting goals not only provides clear focus but also significantly increases the degree to which employees feel engaged and committed to achieving the goals.

More than just knowing expectations, employees need to know the *why* behind them. Knowing the big picture and understanding the relevance of a task is not simply something nice to do. The more information the employee has, the more he or she knows about how the assignment fits with the overall game plan and the better decisions he or she will make, especially when problems arise. Understanding the importance of something that may appear of little importance can make a big difference. For example, about twenty years ago several horses in New Jersey died from poisoned grain. The grain was traced to the production facility and a single batch. It turned out that the vats that held the grain had not been properly cleaned between the production of chicken and horse feeds. Medicine put in chicken feed is poisonous to horses. Having no idea of the consequences, the employee responsible for sterilizing the vat between batches decided to take a shortcut. Unfortunately, all too often employees and supervisors understand the importance of explaining why a task matters only after a problem arises.

Goals and expectations need to be written down. They should be spelled out in terms of what success means. For example, "Successful completion of this goal means that by December 1, with a budget of $10,000, you will decrease quality defects by 3.5 percent without any resulting increase in production costs." Potential barriers, such as a lack of training, tools, resources, and, critically, buy-in from others, should be identified and addressed up front. Failure to engage others relevant to the project—including shift supervisors, production schedulers, line employees, and maintenance—will almost certainly lead to problems.

Be Specific When Setting Expectations

Among the most important actions you can take to increase productivity and efficiency in your organization is to create checkpoints and have people work to deadlines. If you want to make sure that something doesn't get done, just tell your employee, "Work on it when you have time." I've got a long list of tasks waiting to be done when I have time. The larger and more complex the task, the more checkpoints you need. At each checkpoint, the employee should know how much progress is expected of him or her to keep on track. If you've ever run a marathon, you know how important it is to see your time at each mile marker; employees also need to know if they are on pace. In our quality improvement example, if the project is to be completed in three months, checkpoints should be set at least every two weeks. Additional checkpoints should be added at the beginning and end, which are typically the most critical times.

Whenever possible, provide employees with physical examples of the desired outcome. Having a picture of what it is supposed to look like (whatever *it* may be) greatly facilitates reaching the goal. If I know what it looks like I can use it as a model; for example, if you expect a report completed in a certain way, provide a sample report. Think about the last time you bought something that needed to be assembled. If you're like me, you threw away the directions and just looked at the picture on the outside of the box. Knowing what something is supposed to look like dramatically increases the likelihood of it turning out that way.

The following story is a clear, although somewhat extreme, example. One of my clients, a very hands-on CEO, recently hired a senior-level executive. During the interview process the CEO was very clear in describing the culture of the organization, which included having a "spotless image." For example, employees are expected to keep their offices and work areas neat and anyone with a company car is required to wash it on Sunday. One weekend the CEO stopped by his new executive's office and determined that it did not meet his expectations. He cleaned the office and left the following note: "When I say that your office needs to be neat, this is how I expect it to look." Although I don't recommend this strategy, the new VP now clearly knows the expectation. If you find that people are often not meeting your expectations, I suggest you start taking some responsibility for being clearer with your communication. What you mean by a clean office may not match up with an employee's definition of one. People who are highly intuitive need to be particularly sensitive to giving vague instructions; they typically have a clear idea of what they want in their head but often don't paint a full picture for others.

Have you ever worked for a boss who told you that you should focus on X one day, changed it to Y a few days later, and the following week asked why you were working on Y when you should be making progress on Z? Such supervisors greatly frustrate employees and inhibit their productivity and efficiency. How can any employee feel fully engaged and committed to reaching a goal when it may no longer be relevant tomorrow? Under these circumstances, employees feel jerked around and often lose respect for their supervisors and feel disrespected. Most goals should be set out several months in advance and altered judiciously for sound and clearly articulated reasons.

I once consulted with a large chain of dry cleaning stores. The owner was frustrated that his shirt pressers were not more efficient; they averaged forty-five shirts an hour, and he wanted them to do sixty. These were very experienced employees, and

I cautioned the owner that such a dramatic increase was highly unlikely without some significant change in the process and/or technology. Nonetheless, I began as anyone would by observing and interviewing the employees. I asked the obvious questions, including, "What would it take to get to sixty shirts an hour?" During these conversations, I realized that the employees had no idea how many shirts they were currently pressing, nor had they ever heard of the sixty-shirts-an-hour goal. Again, the primary reason that most goals aren't met is that they are not clearly defined and communicated.

The intervention was simple; I had the manager at the processing plant hang a large whiteboard and graph the production rate every hour for a week, during which productivity increased each day as employees got feedback on their performance. By Friday, they averaged fifty-six shirts an hour. On the following Monday morning, I facilitated a meeting with the plant manager and employees during which we reviewed the data and asked for suggestions on how they might be able to reach a steady production rate of sixty shirts an hour. A few very simple changes were made based on these suggestions. For example, children's shirts were particularly difficult to press, but one employee worked on a smaller press that handled these shirts best, so children's shirts were redirected to her. Employees now press an average of sixty-five shirts per hour.

As you can imagine, this experience led to several positive outcomes for the employees, manager, business owner, and customers. First, because of the increased productivity, the owner could offer customers same-day service on all shirts, which led to a competitive advantage in his market. Second, he reduced his employees' hours but raised their pay. Third, because their manager had actually listened to and acted on their suggestions, the employees' level of engagement increased, which in turn led to more input and various improvements and cost savings.

Perhaps the most important outcome was the transformation of the relationship between the manager and his employees. Before this experience, the manager had run the operation as a dictator might his country. He was very authoritarian and interested only in employees doing as they were told. Now, they share a much more collaborative and respectful relationship. He no longer had a workforce; he had a team. By the way, turnover, which had been a significant problem, has decreased dramatically. If your employees are not meeting expectations, maybe it's time for a conversation.

Best Practices and Turnkey Strategies for Setting Expectations and Goals

It is in your best interest to make sure that you and your employees are on the same page. Setting clear expectations should begin during the hiring process and continue throughout the length of the employee-manager relationship. The following are some concrete structures to help you on your way:

1. **Real deal.** During the interview process, most job candidates are not given an accurate description of the job and what to expect from the organization. Thus, candidates end up with an airbrushed version of what to expect instead of the "real deal" and become naturally disappointed shortly after accepting the job. As part of your interview process, job candidates should have time to speak individually with

current employees and should be encouraged to ask questions regarding what it is really like to work in this organization; employees should be encouraged to be honest and forthcoming in their responses.

2. **Set expectations early.** One of the most critical conversations for supervisors to have during the interview process and immediately after an employee has been hired revolves around expectations—both what is expected from the employee and what he or she can expect from the supervisor and organization. Employees should be given a detailed accounting of goals and objectives for the upcoming twelve months—not just a job description. As part of the interview process, supervisors should actually go over performance evaluation forms so candidates know exactly the criteria on which they will be evaluated.

3. **Measure it.** In psychology we say, "If you can measure it, you can change it." Putting objective measures into place allows employees to constantly assess their progress relative to the goal. Real-time performance feedback increases the likelihood of achieving any goal. The process need not be complicated—for example, hourly production numbers written on an easily accessible whiteboard. My favorite example comes from Binney & Smith, the makers of Crayola Crayons. After giving a talk on the RESPECT Model, I was given a tour of the manufacturing plant. At each workstation was a small flagpole that flew either a green or a red flag. The green flag meant that the team at that station was on or ahead of the production schedule, while a red flag indicated that the team was behind. In the center of the plant was one large flagpole; when all team flags were green, it flew a large green flag. Thus, anyone would instantly know the status of individual teams and the team as a whole. Naturally, no team wanted to

be flying a red flag. Moreover, when a team got behind, someone from a green team frequently offered assistance. Great organizations have great practices.

4. **Write it down.** Whenever delegating a task, make sure to put in writing all relevant expectations and instructions. Have you ever had someone make a request and ten minutes later you forgot the specifics? If I don't have it in writing, chances are I'm just not going to remember. Moreover, I tend to be embarrassed that I forgot, and instead of bothering the person and potentially looking incompetent, I will simply take my best guess. *Never* assign a task or set an expectation without having it in writing.

5. **Check for understanding.** Make sure the employee "feeds back" the expectations. Never say, "So you got it?" because whether they do or not, your employees will likely say yes. Instead, try saying, "I'm not always as clear as I should be, so could you please repeat back what you heard me say?" Another effective strategy is to have the conversation and then ask the employee to reiterate the request in a follow-up e-mail.

6. **Put checkpoints in place.** Right from the beginning of a project, establish checkpoints by time and major project targets. You should have more checkpoints early in the process because the consequences and impact of making a wrong turn early are significant. For example, if you're driving to your Aunt Linda's for Christmas and start out on 95 North instead of 95 South for a hundred miles, you're in a lot worse shape than if you make a wrong turn on a side street within a few blocks of her house. At the same time, you probably want to be particularly attentive to the details at the end of the project; those last few turns can be tricky. By building

in checkpoints up front, you eliminate any potential awkwardness when you check an employee's work. You also create a natural opportunity for employees to ask questions and clarify points that they otherwise might not have wanted to bother you with.

7. **Set goals collaboratively.** Telling an employee what needs to be accomplished versus reaching those expectations in partnership significantly impacts the employee's level of engagement and the extent to which the goal is achieved. Setting goals with employees should be a conversation, not a demand. For example, instead of saying, "You need to get five new accounts by the end of the month," you might say, "I wanted to have a conversation with you about your sales goals" and ask the employee for his or her thoughts. In most cases, the employee's goal will be realistic and very near the one that you would have set. This process leads to much greater ownership and commitment by the employee.

8. **Compare expectations.** The following is a simple and powerful exercise that I encourage you to do regardless of how effective you feel you are at setting clear expectations. Hold a team meeting and tell employees that you want to make sure that you have been doing a good job in effectively communicating your performance expectations to them. Hand out a blank piece of paper and ask them to list in order of priority what they believe you expect from them. In addition, for any task they are currently working on, ask them to write down a score from 1 (Failing to meet expectations) to 5 (Exceeding expectations) for their performance. In advance of this meeting, write down your expectations and evaluation scores. Collect their responses and then hold one-on-one meetings to discuss how closely aligned you are. There is absolutely no

downside to this exercise. If you are closely aligned—great! More likely, however, you will have the opportunity to address differences in perception and provide important guidance. By the way, if you and an employee are strongly misaligned, you should start off the conversation by apologizing and accepting responsibility for not being a more effective communicator. Regardless of the degree of alignment, end all such conversations by encouraging employees to come to you whenever they have questions about expectations or how they are doing.

9. **Expect great things.** There is an old saying, "You get what you expect," and if you don't expect much you won't get much. One of the best signs I ever saw in a manager's office read: "I expect great things from you; please expect the same from me." I find that if you see people as great, they do great things. Set challenging goals that let your employees know that you have confidence in them. Most people resist setting higher goals because they fear failure. You should foster a culture where the only way people can fail is if they don't try to improve. Obviously, you need to be a role model. In fact, I encourage you to write your goals on a whiteboard in your office, track your progress, and encourage your team to hold you accountable.

10. **Manage expectations.** Employees frequently speak about having learned how to manage their boss's expectations. Sometimes this is done in the spirit of manipulation when employees believe that they have "trained" their supervisor to lower his or her expectations. Obviously, such manipulation should not be tolerated. However, employees should be encouraged to keep in regular contact with their manager and keep him or her apprised of any possible concerns. It is far more desirable to manage expectations than to allow others to believe that projects are on track when they are not.

"I'm Confused and I'm Concerned"

Several years ago, I started using the expression "I'm confused and I'm concerned" whenever someone failed to meet an expectation. For example, "I'm confused because I thought that I was clear in my expectation that the report would be finished by 5:00 today, and I'm concerned because that expectation does not appear to have been met. Please help me understand." I always want to leave open the possibility that I was not clear in my communication or may have misperceived the situation in some way. Critically, this approach avoids the other person immediately becoming defensive and promotes a sense of collaboration.

The Bottom Line

It doesn't matter how well trained your people are—if they don't clearly know what is expected of them, they are going to miss the mark. Supervisors who collaborate with employees to set clear goals show respect to their employees and foster a culture of engagement. A word of caution: all goals should be viewed as checkpoints on the path of continuous improvement. Never allow a goal to create a "ceiling effect," where there is no room to grow. In other words, don't let goals limit what is possible for you, your employees, or your organization. In the next chapter we tackle the most difficult to teach driver in the RESPECT Model: consideration.

CHAPTER 10 Consideration

"People do not care how much you know until
they know how much you care."

—*John Maxwell*

Showing consideration to employees is one of the
quickest, easiest, and most effective ways to
increase employee engagement. *Consideration*
refers to giving careful thought to a person or idea and is demonstrated through one's words, decisions, and actions. People differ considerably in their ability to be considerate, which requires empathy and an understanding that others have feelings, needs, and beliefs separate from one's own. While empathy is perhaps the most critical innate skill for a leader to possess, it is nearly impossible to teach, since it is so closely tied to personality. Moreover, those who lack empathy typically dismiss it as not being an important leadership skill.

Time and again, research participants shared stories of considerate acts by supervisors that demonstrated the impact of consideration on respect, engagement, and loyalty. Among the many diverse stories, the most common theme involved a personal or family health issue.

The following story is quite personal, as it involves my wife, Karen. She was living and working in New York City when her mother, Violet, was diagnosed with pancreatic cancer. Violet lived in Long Island and needed transportation downtown to Sloan Kettering every Tuesday for twenty-four weeks. This meant that Karen would have to leave work at noon to make the round-trip to Long Island. Karen presented the situation to her boss, who without hesitation told her to take care of her mother. He trusted her to make up the lost hours and never docked her vacation or personal time. In Karen's words, "At the most difficult time in my life, I was blessed to have a kind and thoughtful boss who let me know that he cared about me as a person and not just as an employee."

One would hope that employers would show consideration in such circumstances simply because it is the right thing to do. However, from a business perspective such situations create unique opportunities to significantly increase an employee's level of engagement and subsequent commitment, loyalty, and discretionary effort. Acts of generosity and consideration are paid back tenfold by employees. On the other hand, if Karen's supervisor had not been so considerate, she would have either quit or become significantly less engaged. By the way, there is also a spillover effect on other employees who observe the decision and imagine being in their team member's position. Thus, Karen's team members had greater respect for their manager and most likely were more engaged as a result of his decision. Being inconsiderate toward employees, particularly when it comes to health and wellness issues, is a terrible business decision.

Of course, being considerate involves many smaller gestures as well, made on a daily basis. Below is a brief assessment that will provide you with a sense of how your employees view your level of consideration. Since this is a particularly difficult driver to objectively self-assess, I encourage you to ask your employees, as well as others with whom you work, to provide you with anonymous feedback around these statements. In the sections ahead, we will take a look at specific strategies for showing your employees consideration.

CONSIDERATION SELF-ASSESSMENT QUIZ

Read each statement below and decide how accurately it describes your behavior using the following scale:

a. Never or rarely engage in this behavior (0 points)
b. Sometimes engage in this behavior (1 point)
c. Regularly engage in this behavior (2 points)
d. Always or almost always engage in this behavior (3 points)

Place the point value of your answer choice on the blank line at the beginning of the statement.

_____ 1. I spend time checking in with my employees every day.

_____ 2. I reinforce team members when I see them acting considerately.

_____ 3. I notice when employees are not themselves and let them know that I am concerned about them.

_____ 4. When employees come in sick, I encourage them to go home and take care of themselves.

_____ 5. I ask employees specific questions about their family members, such as, "How is your son John doing in soccer?"

_____ Total Number of Points

INTERPRETING YOUR SCORES

0-5: Your employees view you as inconsiderate and uncaring. Your lack of consideration is adversely affecting your employees' experience of feeling respected, which in turn decreases their level of engagement and, subsequently, the success of your organization. Your ineffectiveness in the area of consideration requires immediate attention.

6-10: While your moderate level of consideration is not actively causing employees to disengage, it is not helping them to engage either. Scores in this range may also suggest that you are showing favoritism to some employees. Make sure that you are demonstrating consideration to all employees—not just to those who are the most productive or with whom you have a close personal relationship. Identify which behaviors lowered your score and seek to improve in these areas.

11-15: You are generally viewed as a thoughtful and considerate leader whose behaviors foster a strong sense of loyalty and commitment from your employees. Your ability to empathize with others will make them feel understood and respected. Consider working to develop other leaders in your organization who lack this skill.

Benefits of Treating Employees with Consideration

Treating employees with consideration impacts their experience of feeling respected and subsequent engagement in numerous ways. Most critically, supervisors who demonstrate high levels of consideration foster employee loyalty, which reduces turnover and absenteeism. Loyal employees "show up" literally and figuratively at work, on time and engaged. Such reliability is particularly important in difficult economic climates when organizations need engaged employees to keep rowing instead of jumping ship or having one foot out of the boat. Loyalty is also the buffer against your most productive, well-trained staff being enticed away by your competition.

Like sports fans supporting their favorite team, loyal employees take pride in their organization. This pride shows up in the quality of their work and overall positive attitude toward the organization. In contrast, we have probably all experienced employees or friends admitting that they think so little of their company's products or services that they use those of a competitor. Obviously, such statements do considerable harm to the reputation of your organization and what it has to offer. By contrast, employees treated with consideration will treat your customers considerately. Employees who feel cared about also treat their team members and supervisors with consideration and respect. Not only does this lead to enhanced team functioning and effectiveness, but it also communicates professionalism to your customers.

Supervisors and organizations show consideration when they ask employees for their input before making big decisions that affect their jobs. Obviously, the impact is much greater when the employees' ideas are actually implemented. Moreover, such decisions are often wiser, as the employees are closest to the work. Of course, involving employees in the decision-making process also leads to a greater sense of ownership and facilitates adoption and implementation of the decisions by the employees. Therefore, up-front consideration has the significant added benefit of greatly decreasing resistance to change.

Any change initiative will be more successful when employees are shown consideration. A classic example is working on an integration project where different people, processes, software, and so forth must be merged. Such projects always foster uncertainty, which leads to fear. In such a psychological state, people drag their heels, are less likely to cooperate, and, in some cases, actively sabotage the integration. Empathic leaders understand these feelings and take time up front to identify and address employees' concerns. They also make sure to overcommunicate every step of the way. When leaders consider the impact of decisions on people and act in considerate ways, transitions go much more quickly and smoothly.

Story from the Trenches

Carlos was a hard-nosed, hardworking small business owner who viewed any personal discussions as inappropriate and detracting from productivity.

I explained the importance of empathy and its impact on employee engagement and consequently his company's profitability. He responded, "Why should I care if someone's dog died?" I interviewed several of Carlos's employees, and it will come as no surprise that most disliked Carlos and did their best to avoid him. My most memorable interview was with Lucy, the company receptionist. She had been with the company only a short while, and I asked her whether she liked working there. She became emotional and said, "The owner walks past me every day and doesn't even acknowledge that I exist. The only time he talks to me is when he wants me to do something. He thinks he's so superior because he owns the company and has so much money. He doesn't care about me and, quite honestly, I don't care about him or this company. As soon as the economy turns around and I can find another job, I'm out of here." As you can imagine, her attitude played itself out in her performance and treatment of company visitors.

Ironically, Carlos was fond of saying, "I don't care if my employees like me, only that they respect me." *Respect earned out of fear isn't respect; it's submission.* Carlos doesn't have followers; he has people who show up to collect a paycheck. Leaders like Carlos believe that if employees like their managers then they won't respect them. This simply isn't true. What is true is that if you don't show respect to your employees, they aren't going to respect you, your organization, or your customers.

Fundamentals of Consideration

Consideration goes beyond simple politeness, which requires only an application of learned behaviors in common situations, such as holding a door open and saying "please," "thank you," and "excuse me." Consideration involves careful thought and deliberation. Opportunities to be considerate are greatly enhanced when supervisors have an established relationship with their employees. Employees who feel connected to their supervisors will feel more comfortable sharing concerns and problems. The more you learn about and take an interest in an employee's life, the more he or she will feel respected by you. Most important, the more thoughtful and considerate you have been, the more likely your employees will be to confide in you under times of personal and professional stress when you can make the most difference.

Knowing about problems is obviously a prerequisite to doing something about them. Supervisors viewed as uncaring rarely become privy to such information and, consequently, have few opportunities to support their employees. To break this vicious circle, begin by asking questions that demonstrate interest in your employees' work and career and build up to more personal inquiries.

Knowing more about employees and their lives also allows supervisors to demonstrate proactive consideration, that is, do something that will be perceived as considerate that is not simply a reaction to a situation. For example, imagine sitting on an airplane reading a magazine. You come across an article about one of your employee's favorite authors and bring it back for him or her. Such small acts make a big impact on employees' experience of consideration, because they demonstrate that you know and remember something personal about your employees and think about them away from the office. Again, the point is that the more you know about your employees, the more opportunities you will have to act considerately. The most obvious way this occurs is through daily conversation, even if just for a few moments. If you don't know what's going on in your employees' lives, you're going to miss most of the opportunities to be considerate.

I find it discouraging that when I ask supervisors and managers to give examples of how they have shown consideration to their employees, most struggle to come up with more than a handful of examples—some cannot even come up with one. Fortunately, research participants shared many excellent examples of being treated with consideration. Because consideration is the RESPECT driver that often presents the greatest challenge to supervisors, I have provided many examples.

Examples of Consideration

• "My boss instituted a policy that unless absolutely necessary, he does not want employees traveling on Sunday night or
getting home late on Friday night. This policy has meant a lot
to me and my family."

• "I work as the administrative assistant for a group of totally
stressed out executives. Most of them call, e-mail, or stop by
frantic about needing something done right away. Mr. V. is different. He is always organized and gives me plenty of lead time
or asks me how much time I will need. When he does need
something rushed, he is always very respectful and apologizes
and says that he understands if I can't get it done."

• "At Thanksgiving, my company handed out complete turkey
dinners to all three hundred employees and their families!"

• "My son's high school football team made the state playoffs.
When my family and I got to the game, I saw my boss and
several people from my office. I was totally blown away. My
boss had arranged it and after the game took everyone out for
pizza. It meant more to me than any raise or bonus I ever got."

• "The economy has really hit our company hard. We've gone
through three rounds of cuts over the past eighteen months.
Everyone is scared and stressed. Throughout this process, our
department manager has been totally straightforward. She
hasn't sugarcoated anything or made promises she can't keep.
She always communicates with us and lets us know that we
can come talk to her anytime."

• "At 4:00 on a Friday afternoon, a client called and said that
he needed me to immediately rerun a report that would take
three hours. I had plans to go away for the weekend with my
boyfriend and promised him that I would be out by 5:00. When

continued

I got off the phone, I let out a little scream. My boss heard me and came out of his office and asked me what was wrong. He told me to get as far as I could by 5:00 and that he would stay and finish it. I was so appreciative."

• "My husband lost his job, and my boss offered to let me pick up an extra shift at work. It really helped out."

• "I'm a schoolteacher and had worked very hard to put together a new program that ended up being cut out of the budget. My supervisor actually came to my house to tell me the news personally and how sorry she was."

• "I work in an old building, and the heating/cooling unit never works right. My boss went out and bought each of us a portable heater/fan and said that it was important to him that we were comfortable."

• "My daughter got pneumonia and needed to stay home from school for a week. I am a single mom without much support and couldn't afford a babysitter. My boss set it up so that I could work from home with a laptop and e-mail."

• "Our boss started an awesome health program last Christmas. She made a deal that for every pound that an employee lost, that employee would receive ten dollars and an additional ten dollars would go to the local food bank. She hired Weight Watchers to come to the office and paid for 50 percent of everyone's health club membership. She took the lead and lost fifty pounds! It was a really great boost to the morale of our whole company."

• "Our company hired a doctor who came around to each of our workstations and watched us work. He then made recommendations like modifying our posture, getting more light, adjusting the chair, and changing the height and position of the computer monitor. In some cases, people got new work-stations. It really showed that our company cared about our well-being."

• "I was feeling totally overwhelmed in my job and just couldn't get all my work done. I was not doing anything well and felt like I was going to crash and burn. I went to my boss, and he told me that he never wanted me to feel like that. He sat down and helped me reprioritize assignments and took some things off my plate. His support made a huge difference, and I was able to be much more effective in my job."

• "I was up for a promotion and didn't get it. I was very upset. Although it is not normal procedure at my company, my boss called a meeting with me, the hiring manager, and the human resources manager. He started the conversation by saying that he took personal responsibility for his employees' development and wanted to know what he needed to do to better prepare me for the next level in our company. It really blew me away, and within a year I had gotten an even better job than the one I hadn't received."

• "Whenever I meet with my boss, she shuts off the ringer on her cell phone and lets her office phone go to voice mail. My last boss used to answer every call and even checked his Blackberry while I was trying to talk to him. It makes such a difference to know that your boss respects you enough to really listen to what you have to say and focuses on your conversation."

Best Practices and Turnkey Strategies to Increase Consideration

Although it is difficult to teach empathy, there are specific concrete strategies that will increase your employees' experience of being treated with consideration. This list is not all-inclusive, and you should work to create and develop your own repertoire of ways to be more considerate. As a starting point, I encourage you to think about times when a supervisor treated you or another team member with consideration. You might even ask your employees directly how you could be more considerate.

1. **Know your employees.** The more you know about a person, the more opportunity you will have to be considerate. Therefore, you want to begin storing up information about your employees. If asking questions and learning about your employees is not natural to you, approach it with the attitude of being curious about the people who work for you. For example, ask yourself, "I wonder what this person enjoys doing outside of work?" The most effective way to store the information you gather is by using a program such as Microsoft Outlook, which allows you to create specific data fields and set calendar reminders. If Outlook is not an option, you can also use Excel, Word, or various online tools such as Google documents. You can even go old school and use oversized index cards.

Regardless of the collection method used, begin by recording the employee's birthday and start date with the organization. Next, record any information that you know about his or her family members, such as names and ages of children. Write down what you know about his or her hobbies and interests. This is the most basic information that you should obtain on every employee. Other data that you may collect over time includes where the employee grew up, the employee's wedding anniversary, volunteer work, and special causes, as well as favorite authors/books, music, television shows, and movies and activities in which their children participate. Don't go out and interrogate your employees to get all of this information at once. The idea is simply to get to know your employees better over time through casual conversation.

2. **Meeting practices.** Meetings often present a great opportunity to demonstrate more consideration to your employees as well as increase efficiency. The following recommendations apply to both individual and group meetings.

- Make it a policy that all communication devices be shut off or set to vibrate mode. Individuals with a pending emergency that may require their attention should notify the group at the beginning of the meeting.
- All meetings begin and end on time—or, better yet, early.
- At your next group meeting, ask your staff if they have suggestions on how to shorten or eliminate meetings or limit who must attend. Emphasize that their time—not your time—is important and you don't want it wasted unnecessarily. Meetings that are held purely for the sake of providing updates should most likely be eliminated altogether and replaced with e-mails or written handouts. Often topics discussed in meetings concern only a subset of those present—sometimes only two people. Don't waste your employees' time by making them listen to discussions that have little to do with them. Sufficiently detailed meeting minutes should allow most team members to stay in the loop on issues that do not directly affect them.

- Make sure that you have a meeting process that allows for everyone to be heard and doesn't allow for people to dominate the discussion. For example, when a question is posed, everyone at the table must have the opportunity to be heard. The identified facilitator must manage those who might dominate the discussion.
- Make sure that you fully understand everyone's points by repeating them back for clarity and capturing them on a flipchart or whiteboard.
- Make sure that you look people in the eye when you are conversing.

3. **Feedback Fridays.** Every other Friday have "Breakfast with the Boss" or "Lunch with Your Leader." Have team members sign up ahead of time, then reserve a conference room and order food and drinks. The purpose of Feedback Fridays is for the employees to bring their concerns, thoughts, and ideas. The supervisor is primarily there to listen, ask questions, and take notes. The key is to follow up with an e-mail, phone call, or personal note within twenty-four hours thanking all attendees individually for participating and addressing their concerns or offering suggestions as appropriate. Without follow-up, there will be no participation.

4. **One-on-one.** Send out an e-mail or announce at a team meeting that you would like to meet with each employee for thirty minutes during which time you will ask them to share their frustrations and concerns. Let them know that all topics are fair game—it could be a concern about a current process, job responsibility, direction the company is headed, even something about your management style or their work area. You want to know what frustrates them. During the meeting, listen, ask questions, and repeat back what you've heard to show that you fully understand their concerns from their perspective. *Do not* try to explain why something is a particular

way; rather, empathize with the employee. For example, if an employee tells you that he feels that the new vacation policy is unfair, you might say, "I can certainly understand why you might feel that way." When people feel that you understand and empathize with their concerns, they feel understood.

5. **Celebrate special days.** Put your employees' birthdays and anniversaries on your calendar and let them know that you remember with a card or personal note.

6. **Wind-Down Fridays.** Make it a company policy that no new e-mails are to be sent out within the organization after noon on Friday, nor should there be any meetings held.

7. **Stop the noise.** One of the biggest complaints that employees have is distraction from others' conversations. If your employees work in open cubicle areas purchase noise-canceling headphones for them. Not only will they greatly appreciate it, but they will remain more focused and productive.

8. **"Get to Know You" Lunches.** Every week, take one employee out to lunch with the agreement that he or she can talk about anything but work.

9. **Coffee run.** One afternoon, go around to each of your staff and tell him or her that you are making a coffee run and ask what he or she would like—it's on you.

10. **Spring for dinner.** If employees are working late, have dinner brought into the office.

11. **Jump-start the weekend.** Assuming your corporate policy allows this type of consideration, let people leave two hours early before a long weekend to get a jump on traffic.

12. **Respectful interruptions.** Ask permission before simply interrupting people while they are working—for example, "May I interrupt you for a moment?"

13. **Don't be presumptuous.** When you call people on the phone, do not assume that they are available and able to speak

with you; it is presumptuous and inconsiderate. Instead, say, "I wanted to talk with you about X for Y minutes. Is this a good time, or should we schedule another time?"

14. **Flexible schedule.** Look for ways to provide flexibility in your employees' work schedule, including working from home. Other than those employees whose jobs require their physical presence, for example, receptionists, security guards, manual laborers, and sales clerks, employees should be able to schedule at least 20 percent of their work on their time. The more flextime employers offer their employees, the more respected they will feel.

15. **Communicate.** Especially in times of stress, overcommunicate. Don't let employees hear news from others if you can share it with them first. Direct, honest communication is the only antidote for gossip, and nothing kills productivity like gossip.

16. **Sincere greeting.** I find it terribly insincere when someone says, "How are you doing?" or "How was your weekend?" Make it a habit each Friday to ask employees what they are doing over the weekend. If you don't trust your memory, write down the responses. At some point before the afternoon on Monday, ask employees how that part of their weekend went. You will be amazed by how much people appreciate such a personal touch.

17. **In the news.** Cut out a newspaper or magazine article on a subject of personal interest to one of your employees and leave it on his or her desk with a yellow sticky, "Thought you might find this interesting."

18. **"Some game!"** Even if you are not a sports fan, watch highlights of the local sports teams so you know who won and lost and can engage in casual conversation with the sports fans in your office.

19. **"Nice picture."** Start a conversation with an employee about something personal on his or her desk, such as a picture of a child or pet, or a piece of sports team paraphernalia. For example, "What kind of dog is that?" Follow up with questions about the dog's name and age; people love to talk about their pets. Ideally, look for an area of common interest with which you can connect and have continued conversation. Sports that are in season are ideal because they lend themselves to ongoing dialogue. As always, make sure not to dominate the conversation; it should be mostly the employee speaking and you listening and asking questions. Don't let the conversation go on for more than a few minutes, and *never* end with, "I guess we better get back to work." Rather, simply say, "It was good chatting with you."

20. **Personal work space.** Encourage people to personalize their work space. If yours isn't, make sure to do so with pictures of your family and pets. Doing so allows people to get to know each other better. Personalized items, especially pictures of family members, also help people remember what is really important and can help lift their spirits when they are frustrated, angry, or depressed.

The Bottom Line

Consider that acting considerately typically costs nothing and pays huge dividends in employee loyalty, which reduces absenteeism, tardiness, and turnover. Unfortunately, those who tend to discount the importance of consideration for employee engagement are also typically those who have low empathy. Even though you may not be naturally empathic, you can practice and act considerately by using the many examples and strategies included in this chapter.

Like consideration, the very last component of the RESPECT Model not only is personality based and difficult to teach but also holds the distinction of being the driver upon which all others must be built: trust.

CHAPTER 11 Trust

> "Few things help an individual more than to place responsibility upon him, and to let him know that you trust him."
>
> —*Booker T. Washington*

Similar to the concept of respect, relationships don't work without a basis of trust. When we trust people, we have confidence and faith in them and their word. Trustworthy people are reliable. Without much thought, we do a lot of trusting in our lives. We trust that our car will start when we turn the key, we trust that our alarm clock will go off in the morning, and we trust that our friends will keep our secrets. In fact, we go through our lives assuming and trusting in hundreds of such things each day. If we did not, we would be paralyzed with anxiety.

Unfortunately, there was a precipitous decline in trust during the first decade of the twenty-first century, particularly in regard to financial institutions, politicians, and big businesses. Most employees no longer believe that their employers will do right by them and, concomitantly, have decreased their commitment and loyalty to their organization. According to research by Gallup, level of trust is a fundamental differentiator of employee engagement. While nearly all actively engaged employees trust their company's leadership (95 percent), less than one-half (46 percent) of actively disengaged employees share the same belief. The more employees trust their supervisor and feel trusted by their supervisor, the greater their level of engagement. To what extent do you act in ways that foster employee trust? Take the assessment below and find out.

TRUST SELF-ASSESSMENT QUIZ

Instructions: Read each statement below and decide how accurately it describes you and your relationship with others using the following scale:

a. **Not at all (0 points)**
b. **Somewhat (1 point)**
c. **Usually (2 points)**
d. **Always (3 points)**

Place the point value of your answer choice on the blank line at the beginning of the statement.

_____ 1. **I trust my employees to do excellent work without me checking it.**
_____ 2. **My employees and colleagues often confide in me.**
_____ 3. **My employees trust me to do right by them.**
_____ 4. **I trust team members to make business decisions on their own.**
_____ 5. **Employees can count on me to "shoot straight" when delivering bad news.**

_____ **Total Number of Points**

INTERPRETING YOUR SCORES

0-5: Your interpersonal style fosters a sense of distrust and disrespect that leads others to disengage from you. Your employees and co-workers do not feel trusted and likely don't trust you. If you are unable to increase the level of trust with your subordinates, your effectiveness as a supervisor will remain extremely limited and detrimental to the human capital of your organization.

6-10: You are somewhat effective in your ability to foster trust among your employees. At the same time, your employees do not feel fully trusted and do not fully trust you. Showing more trust to employees will be recognized as highly respectful and lead your employees to demonstrate significantly more discretionary effort as their level of engagement increases.

11-15: Congratulations, your trust of others and their trust in you indicate high levels of mutual respect. Employees will display high levels of discretionary effort because you have created a culture that shows that you believe in their abilities and judgment. Continue to identify and provide employees with even greater levels of responsibility and autonomy.

A reminder about interpretation of your scores, which applies especially to the driver of trust: As humans, we tend to overestimate good or desirable qualities and personality characteristics; this phenomenon is known as the *illusory superiority* or *better-than-average effect*. In other words, when it comes to self-evaluating traits such as intelligence, attractiveness, sense of humor, and trustworthiness, we score ourselves higher than we deserve. Therefore, as with the previous driver, consideration, I would encourage you to have your team members and co-workers provide you with anonymous feedback to the statements above. It's better to know the truth than operate from an inaccurate perspective.

Benefits of Trust

Trust impacts an organization's bottom line in several ways. As employees experience higher levels of trust, they feel more respected and have more respect for their supervisor and organization, which translates into increased discretionary effort and greater productivity. Employee-supervisor relationships with high levels of trust also lead to greater creativity and initiative, as employees feel safe being innovative and taking risks. While trusting relationships provide an environment that encourages employees to be innovative, environments characterized by distrust eliminate initiative for risk taking and innovation. Employees who are micromanaged will rarely go beyond precisely what is asked of them.

When people trust one another, there is an open sharing of information and resources. In a culture of distrust, people horde resources for fear that others might use them to their advantage. Similarly, employees are more willing to share ideas and collaborate when they trust one another and trust that their ideas will not be belittled, held against them, or stolen. The question "Permission to speak freely?" asks whether one may speak directly without fear of retribution. Naturally, the free sharing of ideas leads to increased collaboration and better decision making. Trusting environments augment improved team functioning, productivity, and efficiency. People who trust one another do not spend time worrying and theorizing about how others' actions might prove detrimental to them. When people distrust one another, they are always asking themselves, "What is he up to now?" Distrust occupies lots of mental real estate better used on productive rather than paranoid thinking.

Of all the RESPECT drivers, none saves as much time as trust. I have seen supervisors who so distrusted their employees that they spent the entire day looking over their shoulders. Not only is micromanagement a complete waste of a supervisor's time, but it actively suppresses the productivity of the employees. Trust also saves time by significantly speeding up difficult conversations; trust allows us to cut through a lot of the pleasantries and get to the point. For example, if we have a trusting relationship, we can have a frank conversation and you will be able to trust that what I am saying is true and intended to help, not hurt, you.

Trusting others facilitates productivity by reducing resistance to change. Especially during times of significant organizational change, such as downsizing, restructuring, merger and acquisition, and sweeping changes in technology, processes, practices, or policies, the extent to which employees trust their supervisor and upper management is a critical determinant of the success of the change effort. Trust acts as a lens that significantly impacts how employees view the decisions of management. The "trust lens" leads people to assume the best, while those viewing situations through the "distrust lens" assume the worst. People resist change primarily because they fear the potential adverse impact on their job. When we trust those implementing the change, we are much less resistant. If you're going through any kind of organizational change, it will be significantly easier if your employees trust the leaders of the change initiative.

Story from the Trenches

Nancy worked as my first graphic artist at ColorMe Company. As you can imagine, this is a highly critical role in a company whose entire product line is based on digitizing children's art- work. Although the rest of the office used computers loaded with Microsoft Windows, she insisted on using her own Apple laptop—which I completely understood and supported. My only request was that on Friday afternoons she back up her work on our computer server. (You know what's coming.)

It was Christmas 2005, and we had decided to invest nearly all of our time and resources into a single marketing campaign. This was a big deal for a small company that counted on Christmas to generate more than 50 percent of yearly sales. Two days before the artwork was due to the printer, Nancy's hard drive crashed. She had not backed up her work in three months. I did not ask her why; doing so would have been like asking a four-year-old why she hit her three-year-old brother—there is simply no good answer.

To say that I was angry and upset at her was an understate- ment. Despite my extreme irritation and disappointment, I realized that firing her at this moment would do more harm than good. It would be impossible to hire another graphic artist and get him or her up to speed before the end of the Christmas season, and there was still work that needed to be done. So I gritted my teeth and began to do what I could to salvage the season.

A few days after this catastrophe while I was working alone at night in the office, I found myself checking Nancy's computer to see what she had accomplished in the last few days. I went home that night with a sick feeling in my stomach; I had to admit to myself that I simply no longer trusted her or her work ethic. The relationship was over. Regardless of how dependent I was on her skill set, I could not have someone working for me whom I did not trust. The next morning I met with her and said, "I am sorry, but it is not going to work out," and handed her a final check. She was stunned and said, "Don't you want to talk about this?" I said, "No." There was nothing to talk about—at least not with her.

After she packed her things and said her good-byes, I called the rest of the team together. I expressed my regret at having to let Nancy go and understood that it might have come as a bit of a shock. We were such a small, close-knit group, and I was terribly concerned about how my team would respond—not just to terminating Nancy but to firing our graphic artist and essentially admitting that there would be no Christmas for ColorMe that year. I felt completely dejected and had a hard time hiding it. I asked if anyone had anything they wanted to say. What happened next was one of the most memorable and meaningful leadership moments of my life. There were three unified responses: first, "We are surprised that you didn't fire her sooner"; second, "What do you need us to do?"; and third, "We will get through this."

As a leader, I matured and learned a lot that day. First, team members know who should be let go before the boss does. Second, eliminating weak team players makes the team stronger. Third, crisis situations bring teams together. Fourth, if your employees respect you, they will respect and support your decisions. Finally, no matter how small your organization, people have to be cross-trained; you simply leave yourself far too vulnerable when only one person can perform a key job function. And there was one more really important thing that I learned from that situation: don't ever let circumstances or fear prevent you from doing what needs to be done.

Fundamentals of Building Trusting Relationships

Like dancing the tango, it takes two to build a mutually trusting relationship, and while you cannot determine whether another will follow, you must take the lead in offering your trust first. In building a foundation of trust for any relationship, there are a few critical things to keep in mind. First, if you're not starting at neutral, you better figure out why and get back there as quickly as possible. For example, if you are moving into a new organization and your reputation is negative in some manner, you should address this up front with your new colleagues and team members. If you cannot clear or reset others' perceptions of you, it will be much more difficult to build their trust. Second, be extremely transparent and overcommunicate—especially when it comes to the processes around which you make decisions. Third, you get trust by giving it. Therefore, it is important when you are in a new supervisory position that you show your respect and trust for those already in the job. A powerful way to do this is by providing employees with greater autonomy and decision-making authority than their prior supervisor. Fourth, let your new colleagues and team members know that you operate from a position of trusting and believing in people and their skills. Let them know that you won't be looking over anyone's shoulder but, at the same time, if they need your support that you are there. Finally, look for opportunities in which others have shown their trust in you and reinforce it. For example, "Thanks, Pete, I appreciate your trusting me on this."

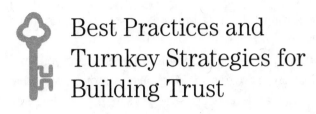

Best Practices and Turnkey Strategies for Building Trust

Below are numerous tactics and strategies that will help you build trust with your team members. As you read through the list, examine your own behavior critically and look for opportunities for improvement regardless of circumstances.

1. **Keep your word.** Follow through on your promises and commitments, including things that may seem small such as calling someone back promptly. On a daily basis, your trustworthiness will be evaluated based on the extent to which you keep your word.

2. **Admit mistakes.** When you realize that you have made a mistake, immediately acknowledge and accept responsibility for it. People may not view you as more competent, but they will view you as more trustworthy.

3. **Give credit.** Make sure that team members are given appropriate credit commensurate with their contributions. If you're going to forget someone, let it be you.

4. **Take the bullet.** When things go badly, take the blame. Shield your employees from fallout and they will be extremely grateful and repay you with trust. This does not mean, however, that employees should not be held accountable for their mistakes or failing to meet expectations. It is perfectly acceptable to protect your employees in public and give them the "confused and concerned" speech in private.

5. **Straight-talk.** When you have bad or sensitive news to deliver, do so quickly in as sincere and straightforward a manner as possible. If your employee hears from others what

he or she should have heard from you, trust will be seriously compromised.

6. **Transparency.** The more open and transparent you and your organization are when making business decisions, the greater the trust and respect employees will have for you and the organization. Leaders who withhold information and cloak processes will be perceived as untrustworthy and distrusting of employees. I cannot think of any business information that should not be shared with employees.

7. **Communicate.** One of the best ways to build trust, especially during difficult economic times, is simply to communicate. In fact, overcommunicate and be proactive about it: send out memos, hold individual and group meetings, publish meeting minutes and weekly updates. The more your employees feel that they are being kept in the loop, the more trusted and respected they will feel.

8. **Confidentiality.** Let others know that they may speak "off the record" and that you will keep it confidential. If you are concerned that a co-worker may be telling you something that you may be obligated to disclose, let him or her know that in advance.

9. **Flextime.** Flextime, discussed in the previous chapter, not only shows consideration by allowing employees to work partly from home or come in during off-hours, but it also earns you points in the trust category. If you want a highly engaged workforce, offer flextime.

10. **Company money.** Nothing shows trust more than allowing employees to spend company money without having to get approval. Depending on corporate policies, create a team rule that any employee can spend X dollars without getting approval. As I said to one of my team members, "If I didn't

trust you to spend fifty dollars, you wouldn't be working here."

11. **Policy audit.** Conduct a policy audit in which you ask employees to identify current policies or procedures that are unnecessary or overly cumbersome. Revise or eliminate as many as possible.

12. **Increase autonomy.** Demonstrate your trust in your employees' skills and judgment by increasing their autonomy and decision-making authority. Hold one-on-one conversations with employees in which you ask them to tell you what additional responsibilities they are willing to accept.

13. **Ask and act.** Ask employees for their suggestions and then act on them. If you don't plan on following up, don't ask. If suggestions cannot be enacted, explain why.

14. **Playback.** When employees come to you with a concern, they are often worried that you will not fully understand their view; they don't trust that you have heard them correctly. To counter this, ask questions, take notes, read the notes back, and ask whether you have accurately and thoroughly captured their concern.

15. **"I don't know."** When we ask someone a question and he or she sincerely responds, "I don't know," it actually increases the extent to which we view the person as trustworthy. It is when we sense that people are making up an answer that they lose credibility and we begin questioning whether we can trust what they say.

16. **Have their back.** Demonstrate that you support your employees and will not hang them out to dry. For example, imagine during a meeting that someone begins to make disparaging comments and questions the work of one of your people. You might say, "I think you are being unfair; he has

always done excellent work and I have no reason to think otherwise now," or "We need to table this discussion until we have more information," or "Let's assume that the work is accurate, and I will follow up with him later." Have your employees' backs and they will have yours.

17. **Trust your employees.** Take your employees' word without questioning or checking up on them. Act in ways that demonstrate that you trust what your employees say to be true.

18. **"I trust you."** If you have delegated a challenging assignment to a team member and he or she comes to you concerned about being able to accomplish the task, say, "I trust you to do this or I wouldn't have given it to you." Obviously, provide the employee with assistance if needed; otherwise you will send the individual off feeling as though you don't understand or care about his or her concerns.

As you go about increasing trust in your relationships, keep in mind that people differ widely in their inclination and approach to trusting others. While some people start from a default position of trust and do so until they have a reason not to, others may require years of demonstrated loyalty and dedication before trusting others. Without question, the opportunity for trust to increase or decrease goes up over time with shared experiences and history. It is as though we have a bank account of trust and can earn points or have points deducted depending on our behavior over time. For example, you can earn trust points when you are straightforward with an employee over a difficult issue, defend an employee's decision during a meeting, or consistently follow up on your commitments. How many points are in your trust account?

Antitrust Practices

Trust is delicate, and you can lose points quickly depending on your behavior. Once broken, mending trust is like trying to repair a porcelain piggy bank; it is unlikely that you are going to get it all back together, and it is never going to be the same. Often, single events such as breaking confidentiality are responsible for shattering trust. However, the larger and more troublesome concerns from an employee engagement and human capital perspective are the ongoing policies and practices that inhibit trust on a daily basis. As already discussed, nothing screams "I don't trust you and your work" louder than micromanaging employees. If you really want to kill initiative and discretionary effort, stand over your employees' shoulders and check their work in detail. Organizations also inhibit trust when they track their employees' behavior through GPS devices and computer monitoring systems, or when they create policies that require additional paperwork simply for the sake of keeping tabs on employees.

Whenever an organization implements or revises existing policies in an effort to correct a performance problem, I can almost guarantee you that the solution is going to cause more problems than it is going to fix. Policies often get implemented in response to an individual or handful of employees with performance issues, which results in penalizing the 99 percent of employees who are following the rules. These kinds of policies end up frustrating your best employees and rarely have any impact on your poor performers, who will find ways around your policies and frustrate you in other ways.

Human nature is such that if one perceives that he or she is being more tightly controlled or watched, that person will pay closer attention to the rules and boundaries so that he or she may figure out how to push or go around them. A good example is when companies block websites such as Facebook in an effort to increase productivity. It should be obvious at this point that such a show of distrust leads employees to disengage and actually become far less productive. Interestingly, a recent study by Professor Brent Coker, from the University of Melbourne's Department of Management and Marketing, found that employees who spent some time surfing the Net were actually more productive than those who did not. Quite frankly, if you are really concerned that employees are spending large amounts of time social networking instead of doing actual work, you have far more serious problems with employee disengagement than any policy could address. In general, any policy that attempts to systematically restrict or track behavior conveys the message that you don't trust your employees. In return, employees will feel highly disrespected and will become disengaged. Remember, in the game of trust, you need to ante up first.

Trust Breakers

Numerous factors detract from or simply break trust in the employee-supervisor or employee-employer relationship. All of them are easy to prevent yet difficult to repair. As you read through the following list, I encourage you to look carefully at your own behavior. Again, since we tend to have blind spots when it comes to our own unbecoming behaviors, I encourage you to seek anonymous feedback from team members and colleagues.

- Lying; any misrepresentation of the truth
- Micromanaging others' work

- Failing to follow through on commitments or responsibilities
- Incompetence; poor work
- Breaking a promise; retracting a statement
- Saying one thing and then doing another
- Talking negatively about someone behind his or her back
- Sugarcoating bad news
- Withholding information
- Incorrectly attributing credit for work done
- Overriding another's decision without explanation
- Manipulation of data or other information, such as creating false reports
- Any form of purposeful deception
- Erratic behavior
- Disregarding or bending a policy
- Covering up mistakes
- Finger-pointing and placing blame for mistakes on someone else
- Allowing employees to believe something you know not to be true
- Making poor judgments
- Making false accusations
- Stealing anything, including customers, resources, or an idea
- Invading privacy, such as searching someone's computer files and logs, listening to an employee's voice mails, or reading his or her e-mail
- Furtively following up with customers or team members to confirm what an employee has told you
- Decreasing autonomy and decision-making responsibility
- Utilizing any kind of tracking or monitoring device, such as GPS or video surveillance
- Restricting access to websites

- Demonstrating or stating distrust of others
- Failing to safeguard confidential information
- Second-guessing one's work, judgment, or decision
- Making decisions that impact a person's job without consultation
- Restructuring implied or actual commitments regarding issues such as health care, retirement benefits, pensions, bonuses, pay increases, vacation time, or work hours
- Any form of unfair, biased, or preferential treatment, such as holding people to different standards, unfair distribution of work, and allowing exceptions for one employee but not another
- Performance reviews perceived as inaccurate and/or not objective

 # Best Practices and Turnkey Strategies for Rebuilding Trust

Most would agree that once trust is broken, it is difficult to repair. Some would say it's impossible. One of the biggest problems with breaking trust is that you may never know what caused it to break, as the offended party may not disclose the incident to you. I suggest that if you see a significant change in the way an employee relates to you (e.g., stops confiding in you) that you have a conversation in which you acknowledge the change in behavior and ask if you have done anything to compromise the relationship.

The following list of strategies can help mend a relationship. It is essential that these be implemented with great sincerity and genuineness. If you really have no interest in repairing the relationship, I recommend that either you or the other person moves on.

1. **Admit that you were wrong and *sincerely* apologize.** Don't try to explain why you did what you did or make excuses. Typically, the other person doesn't care about the explanation. If, however, there has been a genuine miscommunication or misunderstanding, time should be taken to clear up the confusion. Even if what happened wasn't your fault, apologize. My grandmother used to say, "It may not be your fault, but it is still your responsibility." For example, it may not have been your call to reduce your employees' hours, but that doesn't mean that it won't impact their trust of you.

2. **Ask for another chance.** Just as you might in a personal relationship, after you have apologized ask the employee to give you another chance to prove yourself trustworthy. Be thankful if he or she does and understanding if he or she doesn't.

3. **Avoid finger-pointing.** As tempting as it may be, don't sell out others in your organization to try to save the relationship. If you start pointing fingers, the employee will just end up distrusting you and everyone else you've implicated.

4. **Make both a personal and a public apology.** It is likely that if you broke a promise to someone, others know about it and the situation has caused embarrassment and hard feelings that reach beyond your relationship with the one employee. Team meetings tend to be the most appropriate venue in which to offer a public apology. You also want to make sure that you invite people to speak with you directly if they have additional concerns.

5. **Engage; don't avoid.** Rarely does avoiding an issue resolve it. More typically, as time passes the individual becomes more resentful and resolute, and the conversation

more uncomfortable and difficult. The sooner you can get the issue out on the table and apologize, the better.

6. **Continuous dialogue.** Ongoing one-on-one conversations and genuine expressions of interest and concern are necessary for an extended period of time. As long as you are in conversation with the employee, you are likely making progress toward repairing the relationship.

7. **Recommit.** Let the employee know that you are committed to keeping promises and to not breaking them. Ask the employee to hold you accountable and point out any discrepancies between your stated commitments and your behaviors.

8. **Ask if there is anything you can do to fix the situation.** If a request is made that you cannot honor, be sure to express your empathy and regret and clearly state that this is not a possibility, while focusing on what is possible.

9. **Be transparent.** Increase transparency by communicating the reasons behind your decisions and by providing employees access to data that they may not have had before. Become as transparent as possible in your business dealings and show employees that you have nothing to hide.

10. **Reevaluate policies.** Tailor policies or make changes in rules and processes that demonstrate greater trust.

11. **Listen to ideas.** Show that you trust and respect the employee by listening to his or her advice and implementing his or her ideas.

12. **Increase responsibility and autonomy.** Look for opportunities to give the employee increased responsibility and autonomy to demonstrate your trust.

13. **Focus on being fair.** Take the opportunity to look across different relationships, decisions, and processes to

find opportunities to be more fair and equitable. Seek to eliminate any source of real or perceived bias.

14. **Be patient.** Understand that it will take time to prove yourself worthy of earning back another's trust. Remain patient and consistent in your behaviors.

The Bottom Line

Of the seven drivers, trust correlates highest with participants' overall RESPECT score. A strong foundation of trust is absolutely necessary in order to experience a sense of respect and engagement. This is true in both personal and professional relationships. If you have identified trust as an area of opportunity for you, focus here first. In the next and final chapter, we will discuss strategies to help you implement the RESPECT Model in order to maximize the human capital of your organization.

CHAPTER 12 **Implementing the RESPECT Model**

When we show our respect for other living things, they respond with respect for us.

—*Arapaho proverb*

While introducing Vince Lombardi prior to his receiving Fordham University's *Insignis* Medal, Red Blaik said of his friend, "He believes strongly that respect is the essential ingredient that cements successful human relations." Great leaders like Lombardi have always understood that respect is a two-way street and that people follow leaders whom they respect and by whom they feel respected. If you look at any list of great leaders, you will find that most come from the fields of religion, politics, the military, and sports; very few come from business. This relative dearth exists, I believe, because most business leaders fail to appreciate the importance of creating loyal followers. The most educated, hardworking, experienced, and brilliant leaders will fail if they do not engage the hearts and minds of their employees with RESPECT. You can only accomplish so much as one person; if your goal is individual glory, focus on individual sports.

Among the great leaders of the world, few have led with more respect or been more respected than college-professor-turned-Civil-War-hero Joshua Chamberlain. The story of Chamberlain's leadership and courage verges on the unbelievable. Fortunately, it has been well documented and preserved, most notably in Michael Shaara's Pulitzer Prize–winning novel *The Killer Angels*, which details Chamberlain's heroism during the battle of Gettysburg and his successful defense of the hill known as Little Round Top.

Grant held Chamberlain in such high regard that he gave him the honor of overseeing the surrender of the Confederate soldiers. In one of the most poignant scenes in American history, Chamberlain ordered his men to stand at attention to show respect to the vanquished Confederate soldiers as they marched to Appomattox Court House—an action for which he would later be criticized but always defended. In 1893, thirty years after the battle, he received the Medal of Honor, and five years later, at the age of seventy, he volunteered to serve in the Spanish-American War but was rejected for duty. He died in 1914 at the age of eighty-five. Joshua Chamberlain made *respect* an actionable philosophy in his life.

Leading with RESPECT

Whether on the battlefield or in the boardroom, people follow leaders they respect and by whom they are respected. As such, respect brings with it great power to influence others and their behaviors. Respected leaders inspire followers to engage in the work that needs to be done to fulfill the mission and vision of the organization. Many leaders, however, assume that respect should be automatically bestowed upon them based on their position and achievements. In truth, leaders must earn respect by treating those around them with RESPECT every day. Unfortunately, most leaders not only underestimate the importance of showing respect to others but also overestimate the extent to which they do so. Given that leaders rarely receive direct and honest feedback from others in their organization regarding their interpersonal skills, they remain ignorant of their behavior and its negative impact on their employees.

Most of us are resistant to the idea that we need to change, because doing so suggests that there is something "wrong" with how we are now. Psychologists James Prochaska and Carlo DiClemente developed the Stages of Change model, which explains the stages that people go through during a change effort. A key concept in the model is "readiness to change," which refers to one's willingness to acknowledge his or her need to change and receptivity to receiving help. The model has been widely used in the field of health psychology to help people change their behaviors around such issues as smoking, drinking, and drug use. Successful treatment depends on increasing an individual's readiness to change, beginning with awareness of the problem followed by admitting that the problem exists. The more that someone comes to accept that his or her current behavior is unhealthy, the more that person will be receptive to getting the help he or she needs.

Working with leaders at all levels, I have found this model extremely helpful for raising their awareness and increasing their receptivity to RESPECT training. As a starting point, I take leaders at all levels through a 360-degree RESPECT Leadership Assessment, which provides behaviorally focused feedback on each of the RESPECT drivers. (For more information, visit my website at therespectmodel.com.) Leaders are often surprised by the results of this assessment and become much more receptive to coaching. As an example, Tim was the president of a midsized organization experiencing turmoil and turnover in its management team. He attributed the problems to current economic conditions, but I was pretty sure it had more to do with his leadership. The assessment results clearly pointed to the disrespectful treatment of his people as the root of the problem. Although Tim found this feedback surprising and disturbing, it made him receptive to RESPECT training and ultimately transformed his relationships with his team.

At the organizational level, I utilize the RESPECT Organizational Culture and Employee Engagement Survey to provide organizations with a diagnostic assessment of their current level of employee engagement and the extent to which their organization fosters a culture of RESPECT for all employees. As with the individual leader assessment, the results of this instrument provide fodder for organizational leaders to recognize opportunities for improvement. When leaders recognize how much they are losing in discretionary effort based on the engagement level of their workforce, and how relatively easily and inexpensively they can make changes to increase engagement, their readiness to change increases dramatically. Obviously, the leadership team must not only understand and support the RESPECT Model at a conceptual level but also "walk the talk" and serve as role models.

The Future of Respect

My father once told me that every generation believes that each subsequent generation is less respectful. It could be that what

passes for respectful behavior changes over time. As new genera-
tions of employees enter the workforce, they will bring with them
different ideas about what it means to treat their team members
and supervisors with respect. For example, responding to text
and e-mail messages on mobile devices during a meeting seems
pretty disrespectful to me, but it has become widely accepted in
many organizations. I suggest that leaders become much more
explicit and intentional in communicating the culture of their
organization and their expectations regarding respectful behavior. In fact, I strongly recommend that it become a component of
your new-hire orientation program. The following story serves
as an example of what can happen when you don't do this and
how you can resolve it.

Story from the Trenches

Danny was an eager, bright-eyed computer guru whom I was
lucky enough to recruit as an intern one summer for ColorMe
Company. His first task was to fix our network, which I had patched
together. On his second day of work, Danny became frustrated and
began to swear. Although I understood his frustration, swearing
was just not part of our culture. The next morning I met with him
and said, "Danny, I need to apologize to you. When you started
here I did not take the time to share with you the kind of culture
we have and how important it is. Yesterday I overheard you swearing, and that just isn't acceptable here." I then shared with him the
document that contained our corporate vision, mission, guiding
philosophical principles, and team rules. He apologized, and it was
never a problem again.

continued

Since that time, whenever I am interviewing anyone to join our team, I begin with this document and let the person know that if there is anything on it that he or she cannot fully support, then this isn't going to be a good fit. Remember, culture drives behavior and behavior reinforces culture. When hiring, your first concern should be to find people who are going to actively support and contribute to your organization's culture. Incorporate discussions about respect and your corporate culture into your interviewing and orientation processes, and if you need to have any "Danny Conversations," do them today.

Respectful Ending

As important as it is to begin relationships with respect, it is just as important to end them with respect. After ten years with her company, a friend was laid off via a group e-mail. Another friend was fired during a team meeting because her boss wanted to "send a message" to the rest of the employees; of course, the message they got was that it was time to find a new job. I have always tried to make my good-byes as respectful as possible and encourage you to do the same in your organization. Other employees are watching, and how you handle people leaving can have an enormous impact on their respect for you and the organization, as well as their level of engagement.

In saying good-bye to you, I'd like to thank you for purchasing this book and taking the time to read it. I created the RESPECT Model to help leaders foster a culture of respect in their organization and, in so doing, increase the engagement of their employees.

My hope is that this book has served and will continue to serve as a resource for you to do just that. I would like to conclude with a quote from a study participant that perfectly captures the simplicity, power, and essence of the RESPECT Model: "If you want the most out of your people, treat them with respect and they will respect and do more for you."

Appendix

"Your Story"

Instructions: The following list of discussion questions is intended to be answered by team members as part of an overall team-building experience. Individuals may skip topics that they do not feel comfortable answering. These questions may be passed out in advance of the meeting or handed out at the beginning. Team members should limit their contributions to ten minutes. After presenting, other team members should be given the opportunity to comment or ask follow-up questions, which the individual may choose whether or not to answer. All team members should be encouraged to identify areas of commonality.

PERSONAL
- Where you were born and raised?
- What are the names and birth order of your siblings?
- What are your favorite sports, clubs, and hobbies?
- What are your children's names and ages?
- What is the best part of being a parent?
- What is the most important piece of advice that you have/will pass on to your children?

- Do you have pets?
- What is the most adventurous or dangerous thing you've done?
- What is the one thing you want to experience/accomplish in your life?
- What is your proudest accomplishment?
- Who is/was the most influential person in your life and why?

PROFESSIONAL

- Can you provide a brief overview of your work history, beginning with your very first job?
- What was your favorite job and why?
- What was your worst job and why?
- Who was your most influential mentor, and what did he or she teach you?
- What is the best career advice you ever received?
- What advice would you give to someone just beginning his or her career?
- What is the best part about your current job?
- What is the most challenging part of your current job?
- What are your professional goals?
- What are your "push buttons"—the things that people do or say that make you see red or become defensive?
- At your retirement dinner, what are three things that you would want others to say about you?
- In terms of your career, if you had the chance to do it all over again, what would you do differently?

What else would be important for others to know to fully understand you?

References and Resources

Adams, J. S. (1963). Toward an understanding of inequity. *Journal of Abnormal and Social Psychology*, 67, 422–436.

Bandura, A. (1977). Self-efficacy: Toward a unifying theory of behavioral change. *Psychological Review*, 84, 191–215.

Barsness, Z. I., Tenbrunsel, A. E., Michael, J. H., and Lawson, L. (2002). Why am I here? The influence of group and relational attributes on member-initiated team selection. In Margaret Neale, Beta Mannix, and Harris Sondak (eds.), *Research on Managing Groups and Teams*, 4: 141–171.

BlessingWhite (2008). The state of employee engagement 2008—North American overview. Princeton, NJ: BlessingWhite.

Boezeman, E. J., and Ellemers, N. (2007). Volunteering for charity: Pride, respect, and the commitment of volunteer workers. *Journal of Applied Psychology*, 92, 771–785.

Boezeman, E. J., and Ellemers, N. (2008). Pride and respect in volunteers' organizational commitment. *European Journal of Social Psychology*, 38, 159–172.

Branscombe, N. R., Spears, R., Ellemers, N., and Doosje, B. (2002). Intragroup and intergroup evaluations on group behavior. *Personality and Social Psychology Bulletin*, 28, 744–753.

Buckingham, M., and Coffman, C. (1999). *First, Break All the Rules*. New York: Simon & Schuster.

Cable, D. M., and Turban, D. B. (2003). The value of organizational reputation in the recruitment context: A brand-equity perspective. *Journal of Applied Social Psychology*, 33, 2244–2266.

Coffman, C., and Gonzalez-Molina, G. (2002). *Follow This Path: How the World's Greatest Organizations Drive Growth by Unleashing Human Potential*. New York: Warner Books.

Coker, B. (2009). Interview with Dr. Brent Coker available at: http://uninews.unimelb.edu.au/news/5750.

Corporate Leadership Council. (2004). Driving performance and retention through employee engagement. Washington, DC: Corporate Executive Board.

Covey, S. (1992). *Principle-Centered Leadership*. New York: Fireside.

Deci, E. L. (1971). The effects of externally mediated rewards on intrinsic motivation. *Journal of Personality and Social Psychology*, 18, 105–115.

Deci, E. L. (1975). *Intrinsic Motivation*. New York: Plenum Press.

De Cremer, D., and Tyler, T. R. (2005). Managing group behavior: The interplay between procedural justice, sense of self, and cooperation. *Advances in Experimental Social Psychology*, 37, 151–218.

Deming, W. E. (1993). *The New Economics for Industry, Government, Education*. Cambridge: Massachusetts Institute of Technology Center for Advanced Engineering Study.

Fishbein, M. (1967). Attitude and the prediction of behaviour. In M. Fishbein (ed.), *Readings in Attitude Theory and Measurement* (477–491). New York: Wiley.

Fishbein, M. (1968). An investigation of relationships between beliefs about an object and the attitude towards that object. *Human Relationships*, 16, 233–240.

Fleming, J. H., and Asplund, J. (2007). *Human Sigma*. New York: Gallup Press.

Gibbons, John. (2007). *Finding a Definition of Employee Engagement Executive Action Report*. The Conference Board Executive Action Series, No. 236.

Harter, J., Schmidt, F., and Hayes, T. (2002). Business-unit-level relationship between employee satisfaction, employee engagement, and business outcomes: A meta-analysis, *Journal of Applied Psychology*, 87, 268–279.

Harter, J. K., Schmidt, F. L., Killham, E. A., and Asplund, J. W. (2006). Q^{12} *Meta-Analysis*. Omaha: The Gallup Organization.

Herzberg, F. (1968). One more time: how do you motivate employees? *Harvard Business Review*, 46, 53–62.

Herzberg, F. (1962). *Work and the Nature of Man*. New York: Thomas Y. Crowell Co.

Herzberg, F., Mausner, B., and Snyderman, B. B. (1959). *The Motivation to Work*. New York: John Wiley.

Kerr, S. (1975). On the folly of rewarding A, while hoping for B. *Academy of Management Journal*, 18, 769–783.

Krzyzewski, M., and Phillips, D. T. (2000). *Leading with the Heart*. New York: Warner Books.

Locke, E. A., and Latham, G. P. (1990). *A Theory of Goal Setting and Task Performance.* Englewood Cliffs, NJ: Prentice Hall.

Macey, W. H., and Schneider, B. (2008). The meaning of employee engagement. *Industrial and Organizational Psychology*, 1, 3–30.

MacLeod, D., and Clarke, N. (2009). Engaging for success: Enhancing performance through employee engagement. A report to Government. London: Crown Publishing.

Maslow, A. (1943). A theory of human motivation. *Psychological Review,* 50, 370–396.

Maslow, A. (1954). *Personality and Motivation*. New York: Harper.

Mayo, E. (1933). *The Human Problems of Industrial Civilization.* New York: Macmillan.

McClelland, D. C. (1975). *Power: The Inner Experience*. New York: Irvington.

McGregor, D. (1960). *The Human Side of Enterprise*. New York: McGraw-Hill.

Molson Coors. www.molsoncoors.com/careers/employee-engagement.

Murray, H. A. (1938). *Explorations in Personality*. New York: Oxford University Press.

Nink, M. (2009). Employee disengagement plagues Germany. *The Gallup Management Journal*. Retrieved 11/17/09 from www.gallupjournal.com. Princeton. NJ: The Gallup Organization.

Prochaska, J. O., and DiClemente, C. C. (1982). Transtheoretical therapy: Toward a more integrative model of change. *Psychotherapy: Theory, Research and Practice*, 19, 276–288.

Ramarajan, L., Barsade, S. G., and Burack, O. R. (2008). The influence of organizational respect on emotional exhaustion in the human services. *The Journal of Positive Psychology*, 3, 4–18.

Reputation Institute. (2009). *2009 Global Reputation Pulse— US Results*. Retrieved from www.reputationinstitute.com/knowledge-center/global-pulse.

Schneider, B., Macey, W. H., Barbera, K. M., and Martin, N. (2009). Driving customer satisfaction and financial success through employee engagement. *People & Strategy*, 32 (2): 22–27.

Simon, B., and Stürmer, S. (2003). Respect for group members: Intragroup determinants of collective identification and group-serving behavior. *Personality and Social Psychology Bulletin*, 29, 183–193.

Skinner, B. F. (1938). *The Behavior of Organisms: An Experimental Analysis*. New York: D. Appleton-Century Company, Inc.

Sleebos, E., Ellemers, N., and de Gilder, D. (2006). The carrot and the stick: Respected and disrespected group members' motives to engage in group-serving efforts. *Personality and Social Psychology Bulletin, 32,* 244–255.

Sleebos, E., Ellemers, N., and de Gilder, D. (2006). The paradox of the disrespected: Disrespected group members' engagement in group-serving efforts. *Journal of Experimental Social Psychology, 42,* 413–427.

Sleebos, E., Ellemers, N., and de Gilder, D. (2007). Explaining the motivational forces of (dis)respect: How self-focused and group-focused concerns can result in the display of group-serving efforts. *Gruppendynamik und Organisationsberatung, 38,* 327–342.

Smith, H. J., Tyler, T. R., and Huo, Y. J. (2003). Interpersonal treatment, social identity, and organizational behavior. In S. A. Haslam, D. van Knippenberg, M. Platow, and N. Ellemers (eds.), *Social Identity at Work: Developing Theory for Organizational Practice* (155–172). London: Psychology Press.

Spears, R., Ellemers, N., Doosje, B., and Branscombe, N. R. (2006). The individual within the group: Respect! In T. Postmes and J. Jetten (eds.), *Individuality and the Group: Advances in Social Identity* (175–195). London: Sage.

Tajfel, H. (1978). *Differentiation Between Social Groups: Studies in the Social Psychology of Intergroup Relations*. London: Academic Press.

Tajfel, H., and Turner, J. C. (1979). An integrative theory of intergroup conflict. In W. G. Austin and S. Worchel (eds.), *The Social Psychology of Intergroup Relations* (33–48). Monterey, CA: Brooks/Cole.

Taylor, F. (1911). *The Principles of Scientific Management.* New York: Harper and Brothers.

Towers Watson. (2008). *Closing the Engagement Gap: A Road Map for Driving Superior Business Performance: Global Workforce Study 2007-2008.* New York: Published by author.

Towers Watson. (2009). *Driving Business Results Through Continuous Engagement: 2008/2009 WorkUSA Survey Report.* New York: Published by author.

Tyler, T. R., and Blader, S. L. (2000). *Cooperation in Groups: Procedural Justice, Social Identity, and Behavioral Engagement.* Philadelphia: Psychology Press.

Tyler, T. R., and Blader, S. L. (2003). The group engagement model: Procedural justice, social identity, and cooperative behavior. *Personality and Social Psychology Review*, 7, 349–361.

U.S. Merit Systems Protection Board. (2008). *The Power of Federal Employee Engagement.* Washington, DC, 2008.

U.S. Merit Systems Protection Board. (2009). *Managing for Engagement: Communication, Connection, and Courage.* Washington, DC, 2009.

Vroom, V. H. (1964). *Work and Motivation.* Oxford, UK: Wiley.

INDEX